GW00725864

PUBLISHED BY OPENLY CLASSIST

PO BOX 10, MCR M19 2XL

1

PAGES 5 - 98

FIRST KNOW YOUR ENEMY

ANDY ANDERSON
FIRST PUBLISHED 1988

NATURAL BORN

CLEANER

KILLS ALL KNOWN GERMS DEAD

INTRODUCTION

In what follows, I will show that today there are two classes in this country, this society, and two classes only. One dominates the other in every aspect of their lives. This dominated class is the working class. It will therefore be shown that the real enemy of working class people, the enemy that keeps them suppressed - is not Capitalism, not the State, not the never defined 'Ruling Class', but this dominating class, the middle class. It will be shown that this class of people can only remain dominant while we let them; that we cannot start to free ourselves and move towards 'the good life' until many more of us fully recognize this enemy.

Those of you who already know this may think it not necessary to read any further. But I suggest it could still be worthwhile to do so since you may come across an explanation, argument, or angle, that perhaps you hadn't considered before.

However, I shall explain how this fact - of who our true enemy is - has been concealed, and how they try to keep it concealed.

From this, the criticism may well arise that I use the term 'middle class' too often. I do so quite deliberately, mainly because all - from the highly influential institutions of schools, the media, the churches, political parties, trade union leaderships, etc., through to almost every so-called left-wing group, whether Trotskyist, libertarian socialist, or anarchist - are involved in concealing this fact.

Some explanations and arguments are also repeated - this too is deliberate for broadly the same reasons. There are also references to political groups and organisations that some of you may either never have heard of, or have already dismissed as useless to us. Try not to get too pissed off with this. I've referred to them, sometimes simply to underline an argument, sometimes to help dispel illusions about them that may still be held by some working class activists.

The word 'emancipation' is used quite often and some may feel that it is a bit dated. Here again, it is used for a specific reason, namely, because it was mostly used with reference to slavery and oppression. These have been the conditions of working class people from their beginning, and continue to be today.

Some of the things explained, you may already know about - for example, the sham of 'democracy', of the Labour Party, and so on - but some readers may not. Either way, I think it is useful to describe and expose again the truth about such things, situations, and conditions, in one place and in this particular context.

Although a number of features of society are touched upon, the areas examined in more detail are restricted to six:

Class definition *

The Uprisings (so called riots) of 1981 and 1984-85 *

The role of the Labour Party *

Education *

The Media - using television as the example *

Africa - particularly the real causes of famine *

It will be noted, perhaps with some annoyance, that a subject not included is that of 'male dominance and the subjugation and oppression of females'. (The term 'females' is used rather than 'women', (a) because we've said 'male' dominance, (b) because the term 'women' excludes female children - who obviously must not be excluded from such discussion). This subject has not been dealt with here since a book on it is in preparation and will be published as soon as possible.

However, the impression should not be got that this subject is any less important. On the contrary, it is of the greatest importance and must be most seriously examined. For although its solution is obviously paramount to the emancipation of working class women - i.e. some 50% of the working class, few of whom appear to be involved in trying to do something about it - it is also paramount to the emancipation of the working class as a whole. Yet fewer still of working class males see its solution as crucial.

What little discussion and writing there is on this question (most of which, incidentally, has been in the last few years) has been done almost solely by middle class women who are concerned only with the oppression of middle class women - in fact, mostly only with their lack of 'equal opportunity' among their class. Hence, the question of class has been, not surprisingly, deliberately ignored by them.

There are other subjects which have been given little or no attention, such as the role of the TUC and the trade unions. The reason is that the one aim here - to explain and stress why it is so virtually urgent for us to recognise who the true enemy is of all working class people - has reached a greater length than originally anticipated, and the discussion of these last-mentioned subjects would not necessarily make this recognition any the clearer, but would obviously make the whole piece much longer still. So the line had to be drawn somewhere.

Our failure to recognize our true enemy is the reason why today we are no nearer to our emancipation - to freeing ourselves - than ever we were. This then - the recognition, the identification, the awareness, the knowing of precisely what and who the enemy is that keeps us suppressed and stands in the way of our emancipation - is the crucial, imperative and essential prerequisite to ridding ourselves of that enemy.

Throughout what follows, the stress will be on the fact that working class people alone can free themselves. Four things are initially required: awareness, confidence, reason and courage. Awareness that it is the middle class who dominate and imprison us; confidence that, provided no reliance is put on any person or section of the middle class, on any of their political parties, or on any of their attitudes and ideas, we can free ourselves; that it is reasonable to fight to do so; and to have courage to affirm, proclaim, and act upon what reason shows to be true and necessary.

I am working class. I left school at the age of 14 with no 'qualifications', and have never attempted since to gain any. This - despite the possible influences of my past political activity - I believe enables me to explain more clearly, in a less jargonized and 'intellectualized' way, what reason shows to be true.

'THE EMANCIPATION OF THE WORKING CLASS IS THE TASK OF THE WORKING CLASS THEMSELVES'

This statement has been quoted many times over the years. But look back over, say, only the last thirty years, and we see that despite all the activity of all those claiming to be concerned with achieving this 'emancipation', despite the millions of words written in hundreds of differently titled magazines, papers, pamphlets, books, the millions of leaflets distributed, the thousands of strikes, campaigns, and demonstrations, indeed despite all the suffering, we, the working class, are no nearer 'emancipation', to freedom, than ever we were.

Why? WHY? The question still gnaws at the minds of some - revolutionary libertarian socialists, anarchists, council communists, or whatever they call themselves - who, to give them the benefit of any doubt, genuinely want and believe they are working for such a goal. It is a question which causes them frustration, disillusionment, despair, and a number of them eventually to give up. Some, whose brains have been gnawed away, join the Labour Party.

Is there perhaps something wrong with the statement itself? Has it been so often trotted out that it has become a platitude - a proverb maybe .... too many rolling stitches gather no broth? It first appeared in the introduction to the Rules of the Working Men's Association (sometimes referred to as The First International, though it was never officially called this) which Karl Marx wrote in 1864. At first, it would appear to be in total contradiction to Marx's strong support for the State and centralized authority. But the fact that many 'liberal' middle class people gladly joined the Association, and others - including doctors, lawyers, manufacturers, army officers, even the Freemasons of Paris - gave it their sympathetic support, shows that this is more probably not the case. The 'liberal' middle class interpreted the statement as meaning that the working class should do things for themselves. They snatched at this interpretation not only because it fitted in nicely with the arrogance of their false praise for the idea of 'self-help', but also because it enabled them to relieve the sometimes nagging feelings of guilt about their position in society (guilt, incidentally, is about all the middle class can honestly feel) and the general superior holier-than-thou attitude of their class to working class people.

And let's not forget that Marx himself was middle class - a comment the significance of which should later become even more apparent, as well as the answer to whether the statement is flawed.

WHO ARE OUR ENEMIES?

So by whom and/or what are we oppressed and exploited - who and/ or what is stopping us from gaining 'emancipation'? It's obvious too that whoever or whatever it is must be our enemies. It ought to be obvious too that, if we are going to defeat them, we need to know exactly who they are. Who then, according to the 'better revolutionaries', are these enemies? Their answer is the same as

the Trotskyists, the International Marxists, the Communist Party - in fact, the Left in general: they are the State, Capitalism, and The Ruling Class.

'THE STATE'? 'CAPITALISM'?

'The State' and 'Capitalism' are not enemies as such; they are the means, the instruments, through which we are 'ruled'; they are, if you like, the weapons of our enemies; they are the agencies of the true enemy, the dominant class. When we are bound with chains, it's not the chains that are our enemy, it's the people who put them on and do all they can to keep them on.

'The State' - which included the judiciary (judges, magistrates, courts, etc.), the police, the armed forces, parliament, the church, prisons, even social workers - was built up, and is continuously being sustained and strengthened, by 'the ruling class' to run society in their way, and to maintain order in it, their kind and form of 'order' guaranteeing, they hope, that they remain 'the ruling class'.

'Capitalism' is an economic system, the development of which really began with the beginning of the so-called Industrial Revolution and the rise of a dominating middle class. They embraced this system because it particularly suited and benefited them - a system that ensured (as it continues to do today) a divided society in which one class (a minority) dominated the other (a majority). This dominating minority, then, is a 'ruling class'. How this domination works, how it is expressed, how, to their own advantage, people of this class influence, condition, brainwash, pressurize, and control the majority, should also become clearer later.

Yet, as already said, the Left always stress that 'Capitalism' is the enemy of the dominated class. They always refer to it as having a life, dynamic, and motivation all of its own, and almost unconnected with humans - indeed, as if it were some kind of animal. There are many hundreds of examples; but just to demonstrate, let's take one from the writings of somebody who once had a good reputation, at least among those calling themselves 'libertarian socialists', Cornelius Castoriadis - who used to call himself Paul Cardan. In his book 'Modern Capitalism and Revolution', published by a group called Solidarity, he says (p.72): "Can Capitalism succeed in so organising itself that it evolves without conflicts and crises?.... Although Capitalism is infinitely more aware of the problems confronting it and has many more means at its disposal than a century ago, its policies are inadequate whenever they have to cope with the reality of today."

'Capitalism' does not organise itself. It is not infinitely more aware of the problems confronting it. Castoriadis' book abounds with statements attempting to persuade us to see an abstract - an economic system - as the devil incarnate whom we should religiously waste our energy trying to destroy. But, as has been said, he is far from alone in this. The energy put into the examination of their bogeyman, capitalism, by lefty intellectuals is probably far greater than that released by a dozen nuclear bombs - and where has it got us? If they'd put the same energy into trying to discover who 'the ruling class' are, would they have come up with the right answer?

SO WHO ARE 'THE RULING CLASS'?

So what about the mysterious third member of this unholy trinity? Who are 'the ruling class'? Now wouldn't you think that, for working class people, the answer to this question is absolutely crucial? For, as was pointed out earlier, if you don't know who your enemies are, how the hell can you set out to defeat them?

Marx

There have been a few rather half-hearted attempts over the years to answer the question. The Solidarity group - perhaps, during its time, the most reasonable of the so-called 'libertarian revolutionary socialists' - had the odd go. One such that comes to mind was an article in their magazine 'Solidarity - For Social Revolution' of August/ Sept 1979, entitled "In Search Of The Ruling Class". It was an agonized (and agonizing!) intellectual squirm desperately concerned with trying to find out who among the 'top ranks' of the middle class made the most important decisions about how society is run, so as to nominate them as 'the ruling class'. No wonder, then, that the 'search' failed - as did all the other attempts.

Ponce Engels at his fathers place

Their thrashing around failed because they see - or rather, try to see - the ruling class as a class separate from the middle class, instead of the truth that they are one and the same.

The Solidarity group, incidentally, tried another tack. They came up with the absurd theory, adopted from the aforementioned Paul Cardan's book 'Modern Capitalism and Revolution' (see p.93, section 8), that the division in society is between "a class which decides and a class which merely executes" - that the class divisions in modern society are more and more divisions between order-givers and order-takers. This, if nothing worse, is a pretty desperate attempt to mislocate the class division. Not surprising, then, that contained within Cardan's conclusions is also the 'theory' - a 'theory', for that matter, to which the whole 'revolutionary' Left are still glued - that there can be no 'victorious revolution' without a 'union' between working class and middle class activists. (See same book, p.94, section 12)

At another point in the Communist Manifesto, Marx says that it is only the proletariat (the working class) who are "a really revolutionary class" and they "stand face to face with the bourgeoisie today". But Engels defined this enemy of the working class in a footnote: "By bourgeoisie is meant the class of modern capitalists, owners of the means of social production, and employers of wage labour."

So the 'good' middle class revolutionary socialists, anarchists, and others of similar species, seize on this definition like ravenous vultures on a carcass in the desert, for they feel it enables them to exclude themselves from the working class's enemy.

But let's bear in mind that - apart from the fact that Karl Marx and his disciple Friedrich Engels wrote the Manifesto nearly 140 years ago - Engels was himself middle class, a wealthy agent in England for his father's big textile business in Germany, and loved fox hunting.

NOTE

(a) The term 'middle class' best describes the class I am concerned with despite the fact that it is no longer in the middle as it once was, i.e. between workers and peasants on the one side, and the nobility (aristocracy) on the other. It took over from the nobility who later ceased to exist as a class.

(b) I also occasionally use the term 'bourgeoisie' for middle class. Dictionary definitions range from 'members of the middle class' (Chambers), to 'the middle class as distinguished from the working class' (Cassells). The term originally referred to artisans and craftsmen who lived in medieval French towns. Up to the late 18th century, it was a propertied but relatively underprivileged class, often of urban merchants and tradesmen.

(c) Those members of the middle class who make decisions about how society is run - including judges, ministers, heads of police and armed forces, of transport and communications systems, and others like those who decide what, how, when, and where things are produced, all of whom depend for their power on being of the dominant class and on having the full approval, support, and encouragement of the vast majority of their class - these I call the 'top ranks' or the 'elite' of the middle class.

WHAT ABOUT THE SOCIOLOGISTS?

Those who profess to study class, scientifically and systematically, who search for patterns of behaviour among people living in organized social groups, call themselves 'sociologists'. Now we don't need to give a monkey's for what bourgeois sociologists think, but for what it's worth, they generally all agree that, in this society, there is no third class separate from the working class and the middle class, which could be called the 'ruling class'.

However, let's remember that 'sociologists' play an important part assisting their class in remaining the dominant one. In this they certainly do get it wrong sometimes; but if they got it wrong all the time, working class people would be that much more difficult to control. Regardless of whether or not 'Sociology' was at one time a purely theoretical system, it is today a practical tool used in social and industrial control - from middle class governments through to multi-national industrial companies. It is a tool used in a great variety of areas, from military strategy to housing, marketing to industrial relations, and from education through to policing.

'Sociologists' are the advisers to their class; they seek to discover the danger points - the signs when working class people's actions and attitudes look to be becoming dangerous to the stability of their class's dominant position. This they do despite the few of them who think they don't, who try to delude themselves (and us!) into believing that they are engaged in what they like to call 'social science research'.

Through this 'social science research' nonsense they have come up with many 'academic' theories of what class is and what sort of people are in the classes, indeed almost as many as there are 'sociologists' who get books published on the subject - books which, in most cases, started out as theses for degree exams. They have produced hundreds of tables and graphs showing statistical results of surveys carried out to discover, for example, what certain people doing certain jobs say in answer to certain questions. They are keen to divide everybody - the whole of society - into 'strata', i.e. into sections of people whom they put under headings such as:

Owners of companies

Chairmen of companies

Directors of companies

Higher managerial, professional, administrative

Lower managerial, professional, administrative

Skilled, supervisory, and lower non-manual

Skilled manual

Semi-skilled manual

Unskilled manual

Pensioners

Remainder

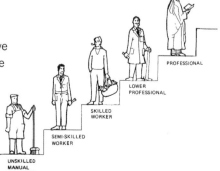

- to mention but a few; and even these are sometimes further divided. The unemployed are generally omitted altogether. So here, before commenting further on the 'sociologists', let's look at unemployment and poverty.

THE CREATION OF 'NEEDS', UNEMPLOYMENT, LOW PAY AND POVERTY

During the period of 'full employment' (i.e. when unemployment was around 2.5%) in the so-called developed countries, the rat-race of 'consumption for consumption's sake' had got well under way. Basic needs (apart from things like housing) had generally been satisfied, and large numbers of people had been manipulated into believing that acquiring this or that commodity would bring them a step nearer to eventually attainable heaven - the proverbial carrots dangled out of reach in front of the donkeys; the standard-of-living hierarchy where there's always another standard to go after, higher than the one you've got.

Then, in the 1960's, despite 'full employment' showing signs of coming to an end, those concerned with the accumulation of profits decided that, if they were to continue enriching themselves, there would have to be more and newer carrots, dangled more vigorously and made to look even bigger, juicier and even more desirable. In other words, they would have to concentrate even more on producing goods which people didn't need, and on 'improving' the techniques of manipulation - that is, training and conditioning people to think they really did need such products, that satisfaction and happiness deepened even more on acquiring them. So more muscle had to be put into the large bureaucratic organisations they use for this - market research, advertising etc.

Much of market research is concerned with finding out, not what people really want and need, but how many can be lured into buying a particular product which they don't need, through 'sophisticated' and 'clever' advertising on TV and radio, in newspapers and magazines etc. It's even done, though perhaps more subtly, through so-called TV entertainment (such as shabby soap operas like 'Dallas', 'Dynasty', 'Executive Stress' and so on) where 'successful' middle class people are seen to have things which the advertisers are pressurizing us all to get.

The range of 'commodities' has no limit; for example, hundreds of millions are spent on similar techniques to push political parties and individuals representing them. A candidate for prime-minister or for president in the USA, is sold (particularly at election time) like a brand of whiter-than-white washing powder. The range runs from houses, cars, holidays through to video-recorders and micro-wave ovens, to thousands of smaller products.

For instance, an 'immaculately-groomed housewife' is shown in a spacious, well appointed kitchen using Brand X to clean the sink. This, in addition to pushing Brand X, puts heavy psychological pressure on women to become similarly 'groomed', a pressure that undermines the self-confidence of those who either don't want to, or for various reasons can't, thus making them feel inadequate and incompetent; and it happens often without them being aware that such 'commercials' are responsible for it - 'commercials', it must

be borne in mind, which are devised, planned, written and directed almost exclusively by middle class males.

Or take a more 'simple' example, deodorants - itself a multi-million pound industry. These are portrayed as a positive and normal desire to achieve what they call personal hygiene - something in which only the deliberately anti-social refuse to participate. This 'desirable' commodity is then split into sub-sections - oral, under-arm, genital, feet - each of which is treated as a separate marketing area, within each of which people can be 'educated' to make choices; roll-on, stick or aerosol; each of various shapes, sizes and fragrances. No doubt soon they'll be something to make all farts silent with smells like lavender, pine, spring flowered meadows...

CREATED 'NEEDS' - ON CREDIT

In the last few years, it has been made easier still for people to get even more things they don't actually need - on credit. In fact, there has been an unprecedented 'boom' in what they call 'consumer spending on credit'; and it's increasing at what a few middle class economists call a truly frightening rate. One such, agonising about it on a BBC documentary 'House of Cards' earlier this year, said that for a lot of people easy credit "becomes a nightmare - people lose their homes, their marriages, even their will to live"

This handful of economists say they are deeply worried about the dangers of 'the consumer boom on credit' because it's being piled up like a blanket, concealing Britains' continued long-running decline in so many other major important fields - and it's now out of control'. Regardless of whether this is so, 'control' is an element in the whole business. More lubrication was added to the wheels of this 'boom on credit' with the introduction of plastic credit cards. But this is not the only reason for them.

Those of us getting 'benefit' - a large section of the working class - receive it in cash every couple of weeks, and we have a little bit of control over what we do with it, like for instance in whether or not to pay the rent, gas and electric bills. Already some of us - council tenants - no longer have the 'choice' of whether to pay the rent, for this is deducted and paid to the local authority without us getting even a sniff of it. But there are now some proposals in the pipeline which would be yet another attack on such small 'freedoms' of that large section. They are proposing to issue cards of some sort - one each for the gas and electricity boards - for the payment of their bills. So it's well on the cards that the time is not that far away when we won't get any cash at all, we'll just get sent plastic cards - including one for the landlord, one for Tesco's, one for... Perhaps then we'll have to somehow increase the number of 'jobs done on the side' - they can't issue plastic cards to pay us for them. But perhaps, before then, we'll take over the gas and electricity boards and British Telecom and the radio and TV networks and the coal mines and Tesco's and...

'Full employment' is gone and will never return - at least for as long as the present kind of society lasts. Yet the pressures on everybody to consume continue and increase. How then is all this affecting the people who, in the 1980's, can't even satisfy their basic needs - those who are on or below the poverty line?

Today there are around 5 million people actually unemployed and the trend is still upward. The official government figure is fiddled to keep it around 3.5 million. There have to date (March '87) been 18 'readjustments' in the methods of calculating the figure since 1979, all but one of which had the effect of lowering, though only on paper, this official figure. Apart from the fact that the many thousands of people conned into the numerous government deceptions ('schemes' they call them in the booklet 'Action For Jobs') are still really unemployed, they are nevertheless excluded from the official figures. Among the devices in the 18th of these calculated frauds (made known at the end of October 1986) are, for example, the exclusion from the unemployment figures of those who have their 'benefit' stopped for not taking a job paying below the poverty-line wages, and/or those who refuse to travel long distances to such a job - and they'll no doubt find other ways to lower the figure a bit more just in time for the election.

Many of the 5 million people actually unemployed have dependents. Even by putting a low average of 1.5 dependents for each person unemployed, it still amounts to 12.5 million people living on or around the poverty-line income due to this reason alone.

Another cause of poverty is low wages. The Low Pay Unit (9, Upper Berkeley St., London, W1) estimates that there are 8.6 million people working for an income which, after deductions (tax, national insurance, travel to workplace, etc.), amounts to the official poverty line or below it.*

Even if - in the case of people on low pay - we take a low average, this time of only one dependent for each low-paid person (and such a 'low average' is taken because, among this number of 8.6 million, there are 3.9 million workers who are part-time, and 60% of all are women), we nevertheless see that there are 17.2 million people living on or below the 'official' poverty line due to this cause.

OVER HALF THE POPULATION IN POVERTY!

Thus, the number of unemployed people and their dependents, added to the number on low pay and their dependents, shows that over half the population of this country - 29.7 million people, the vast majority of them working class - are living in or below poverty line conditions. And that is excluding the third main cause of poverty, old age.

There are millions of elderly people - whom they categorize as 'old-age pensioners' - living without sufficient food and heating, that is, in miserably austere conditions when they ought at the very least have adequate food and heating. This alone is a situation we must hate the dominant class for - a hate at least as fierce as that for any of their other rotten and depraved actions.

Almost all these millions of impoverished working class people are subjected to the intense pressures involved in the creation of 'needs'. They too are continually pressed to believe that to buy! buy! buy! will make life so much better. Telling people that what they really need is something that is impossible to get, causes various psychological problems for them. A few may for a time be able to overcome these problems by kidding themselves - 'I will be able to buy X when I get a job,' or '..... when I get an increase in wages.' But most will not.

It is the first time in history that such a situation has existed. Are these millions of people always going to lay down and take it? Or will it at some point become intolerable? Will they then do something about it? If so, What? When? How? Finding the answers to these questions are problems for the dominant class themselves. They are problems that are already being thought about and plans being made to deal with - particularly by the Home Office and top management in the police.

One thing is certain, the situation for working class people in Britain is worsening and will not get better. At some point in the next few years we are likely to be faced with an upheaval of considerable proportions, and of revolutionary potential for working class people. Will enough of us know at that time who our real enemies are?

★ HOW THE L.P.U. GOT THE CONSERVATIVE FIGURES

A poverty-line income is assumed by the government to be that from Supplementary Benefit. The Low Pay Unit defines low pay as an income which 'translates' into an equivalent of this 'official' poverty line and below. The Unit's figure of 8.6 million is derived from using official data on earnings (which incidentally, show that over the years, the number of people on low pay is increasing) and is, what they call, a 'conservative figure' due to the fact that one in five employers (20%) did not return completed questionnaires asked for by the government through their Department of Employment 'New Earnings Survey' - and it is certain that most, if not all of this 20%, did not return the questionnaires for the obvious reason that they were particularly low-payers.

'SOCIOLOGISTS' **AND** 'SOCIALISTS' OBSCURE THE ISSUE

But to get back to the 'sociologists'. That they divide people into 'strata' is not surprising when you recognize that every activity - including 'educational', commercial, industrial, political, religious, 'artistic', and of course that in every part of the State and the media - is subject to this kind of division: hierarchical division. So everywhere we have a hierarchy - a graded, ranked, pyramid-like structure. It's like a suit of playing cards where every card between top and bottom is superior to those below it, and an inferior of those above it.

HIERARCHY - AN ESSENTIAL METHOD OF CONTROL

Hierarchy is itself an absurd monstrosity. It creates divisions antagonisms and enmity among people, as well as smugness, conceit, aggression, arse-licking, and many other sordid things; and the by-product of all this is that it creates enormous wastage of resources and energy. It can only be defended by the middle class, and they can only justify it as a method of control.

The hierarchical way of organising fragments us and divides us working class people. No wonder, then, that every possible means is used to pressurize and persuade that it is the only way. It is in fact the only way of organising (SOCIETY) to ensure the dominance of the middle class over the working class. Indeed, every society in history that had a dominant minority had a hierarchical structure throughout.

Some appear to have begun to see through the hierarchy device, e.g. the women's support groups of the miners strike. But there's not much evidence that any significant number have, and this is one of the major problems involved in 'the emancipation of the working class' (OUR CLASS).

Thus we see 'management' divided into chairmen, vice chairman, directors, assistant directors, managers, under managers... right through to 'unskilled workers' being divided into head foreman, foreman, underforeman, and so on. This dividing into grades ('strata') fogs over the absolute fact of the true divisions in society.

But the so called revolutionary left - whether libertarian socialists, council communists, anarchists... or Trotskyist groups like the Socialist Workers Party, Militant Tendency, Workers Power - are also guilty of obscuring the issue. Read any of their publications and you will generally find that, according to them, the middle class are virtually innocent bystanders in the class struggle which is solely between 'the ruling class' and the working class; and of course, the same applies to the others of the left such as the Communist Party and the Labour Party. They give the impression that they know exactly who the working class are, but who 'the ruling class' are seems to be an insoluble problem for them.

What was said earlier must be stressed, namely that on the rare occasions when they do attempt a description (analysis they call it), they at best simply describe the 'top ranks' of the middle class hierarchy as if they were a class on their own. It suits middle class 'revolutionaries' - just as it suits the middle class liberals - to get us to believe what they try so hard to deceive themselves about; that these 'top ranks' are 'the ruling class'; 'top ranks' over whom they and the rest of the middle class have no control; 'top ranks', an elite, whose ideas - cultural, social, economic, etc. - are different from those of the rest of the middle class. For if we can be persuaded to believe this, we will not see them and the rest of their class as our enemy.

Their definition of the working class is also flawed, and for fairly similar reasons, for they include in it large sections of the middle class, such as school teachers, social workers, welfare officers, etc.

So they don't know who the working class are, and they don't know who 'the ruling class' are. No wonder their attempts at implementing their theories have at no time brought us nearer to 'emancipation'.

It must also again be stressed that one of the main reasons for the failure of the so called left - a failure which in turn has created confusion and apathy among working class political activists, and consequently among working class people in general - is that the majority of people who run these organisations are themselves middle class, the anarchists included (Peter Alexeivitch Kropotkin, one their main mentors, was a member of the nobility; Mikhail Alexandrovitch Bakunin, another, was middle class).

We can understand the predicament of those among them who genuinely do want to change the power relationships between the classes as opposed to those among them who want to retain some of power - through their political party or whatever - for themselves. Their predicament arises from their inability to overcome their feelings of guilt that they belong to the dominant class - the class whose well being depends on the suppression and exploitation of the working class.

Try as they might, they can't get out of it, they can't become working class. I have seen many times the pathetic and ridiculous antics some of them will get up to (in dress, speech, behaviour) so as to try to feel like and/or be taken for 'working class'. Some, for example, will move into run-down working class areas and live on low incomes, yet never can they experience what it is to be working class because, in almost all cases, they can get out of it, even if only because as with several I have known - there's always rich daddy and/or mummy to help. In any case, virtually all their friends from home, school and university, are middle class and are always there to help by giving them a loan, finding a job or even just a 'good reference', whenever necessary - so they've always got a nice pillow to fall back on. Whereas the working class as a whole have no such 'pillow'; they just can't escape.

WORKING CLASS OR MIDDLE CLASS?

A survey carried out by 'sociologists' a few years ago (see 'Social Analysis of Class Structure', Tavistock publications), showed that working class people themselves are not so confused. It found that 93% of workers in this country (97 % in Sweden!?) believe we live in a class divided society, 80% of whom saw the division as between working class and middle class. (Swedish workers saw a more 'stratified', division.) In reply to the question of which class they belong to, workers here were clear; around 80% said working class, including the few who said 'lower' or 'poor' class. (In Sweden, about 40% saw themselves as working class.)

The 'sociologists' didn't say which workers were surveyed, why the surveys were carried out, nor the reasons for asking such questions. But we do know that the 'sociologists' know what is required of them. They are playing their role; they are keeping tabs on the situation, keeping their shitty fingers on the pulse, testing to see how effectively the psychological conditioning is functioning. (Perhaps the figures suggest that it's functioning OK in Sweden?)

However it ought to be obvious that - inevitably in a class divided society - there can be no clear-cut line between working class and middle class. A few people do move from one class to another; this 'area' is what the 'sociologists' refer to as 'the blurring of class lines'. And it is this small number of people in the 'blurred area' whom many of the middle class left (including the 'revolutionaries') often point to in their desperation to show that the middle class are not the main enemy of the working class. It is nevertheless that the very few working class people who somehow get themselves into middle class jobs - for example, who become teachers, computer-programmers, welfare officers, supermarket-managers, and such like - almost always still behave like working class people; that is, they don't mix socially with middle class people.

Perhaps you've come across the person - usually middle class - who points to someone and, with a note of triumph, says: 'Ah! but what about her/him? What class is s/he?' the important thing here is that we are not at all concerned with the odd blurry individual whose class it may not be easy to be sure about. It is quite easy to see the great majority of the middle class for what they are.

Yet some working class people do seem to have a problem in deciding who is working class and who is middle class. Well, perhaps they ought to ask themselves why they have such a problem. However, there are some guides that may help them. If a person is classified as unemployed, and has been for some time, it's a pretty safe bet that s/he is working class. But of course that may not help with people classified as 'housewives'; nor do 'housewives' come into what maybe the next best guide, occupation. It's generally clear what class TV-studio-cleaners are as compared with those who make, present, and perform in, the programmes; or those who mine the coal and those who manage the industry. Income is a fair indication of class in many cases, but there are some where income alone is not; teachers, the vast majority of whom are middle class, have a smaller income than some working class people in other occupations. there are of course other indications: education, background, parents, life-style, the way they speak, accent...

Anyway, if you've still got the problem; if the 'conditioning' to see class either as irrelevant or unimportant has still got it's grip on you, well don't worry about it. It may clear up eventually and get better - then, if you want to, you'll be able to join with our class in the struggle against our main enemy, the middle class. The point made earlier can't be over-emphasised: we are concerned with the middle class as a whole, not nearly so much as whether a particular individual person is middle class or not. That question only arises when a working class group, devoted solely to the 'emancipation' of our class, is being formed - a question which is returned to at the end of this book. And if, at the time of such a formation, the class of someone who wants to join can't be decided, you could reasonable give her/him the benefit of the doubt, that is call her/him working class - at least until it should ever become obvious that this is not so, then get rid of them.

PSYCHOLOGICAL CONTROL

The problems facing us are of such magnitude that some politically active working class people become sceptical about ever being to solve them and turn despairingly to the originators of many of the problems: 'revolutionary parties', 'vanguards' and 'leaders'. They seem to become blinded to the fact that these have only, can only, will only, sustain and perpetuate the present 'leaders and led' situation.

To others, the degree of control which the middle class have over working class people appears now to be so complete that the abandon belief of ever being able to break it; hence, some seek to modify it, i.e. having abandoned fundamental 'revolutionary' change they go for reforms within the system, for example, through the Labour Party.

The Labour Party, despite it's apparent links with the working class, is a middle class party and has played a very important role in strengthening this control, continues to sustain it, and underpins the middle classes psychological control. Further on, the Labour Party and it's role is described in more detail, but here we'll look briefly at this particular kind of control.

The necessity of psychological control flows from the obvious fact that a society in which one class dominates another can only function so long as the dominated class accepts it's position. If substantial numbers of working class people were to begin to see the true role of, say, the police (a good indication of the degree of class consciousness); were to begin to see more clearly that it is middle class people who dominate their lives; if they were to begin radically criticising the nature and reasons for the existence of hierarchy - in production, education, leisure, and in the various other areas where it ensures control - then the middle class could not remain dominant for long.

If their domination is to continue, it is necessary that the working class not only accept their situation - believe that it is as it should be, or at least that there is no other way - but also that they eventually lose even whatever awareness they have of being a dominated class. If this psychological conditioning could be substantially achieved, the division of society into two apposing classes would become legitimate in the minds of the dominated, a fact of life, and they would no longer see it as something imposed on them. They would then - as some already do - reject as 'wishful thinking' the very idea of emancipation.

A number of working class people who appeared to be aware of the division were asked: 'Do you think it's right that a certain class of people should be better off, that they should decide what is produced in the factories, how schools are run, what you see on TV, hear on the radio, read in the newspapers... should have so much say in the running of society?' Some replied on the following lines: 'It's just the way things are', 'That's how it's always been', 'They're used to running things', 'They're more intelligent.', 'They know best'. This is one way in which working class people try to rationalise - try to defend their subordinate position.

In fact, subordinate does describe their position adequately, for it means: to be in a position that is under others, that is inferior in rank, importance, and power. This, while true of the working class's position - conceals the fact that the middle class has also always sought to subjugate them. That is, to bring them into a state of permanent submission, to enslave them. And although this has by no means been completely achieved, the middle class still keep trying, for they still believe that the 'good order' of society can not be properly maintained unless a substantial number of the working class are submissive and act in a subordinate capacity - a theory, incidentally, basic to fascism which, in Germany, resulted in the concentration camp* and the horrific systematic murder of six million people.

* CONCENTRATION CAMPS

Concentration camps are large areas set aside for the detention without trial of anybody that the 'authorities' decide possesses some kind of threat to them and their class, and for/or whom they can use as scape goats to blame for, and distract attention from, the general harshness of their regime - as was more the case with the Nazis* as far as the Jews concerned. They were first established by a British middle class government during the South African (Boer) wars of 1880/81 & 1889-1902, and since by various other regimes. Today, the 'H' Blocks system of imprisonment set up in Northern Ireland by the British Government also qualifies as a concentration camp.

* An abbreviation for the Nationalsozialistische Dutsche Arbeiterparei: National Socialist German Workers Party/The Fascist Party.

Auschwitz: the sinister motto on the gates of the death factory means "work makes free"

THE 'DEMOCRATIC' SHAM

But, say the middle class, our 'democratic way of life' triumphed over that. 'Democracy', they say, insures against fascism. Does it? You wont have to look far around the world since and in the 1980's to see fascist regimes and there generally propped up by the Western 'democratic' governments! The majority of middle class people, particularly those in the 'top ranks' and in the 'leading' positions of their societies, continually mouth off about their 'democracy' and the crucial need to defend it - a 'democracy' which, just a short while ago, they claimed to be defending when they used such barbaric methods in, for example, Korea, Vietnam, Chile and today Nicaragua, as well as the Botha regime in South Africa. There is no limit to the way they distort language to justify actions that are the opposite of even the false 'democracy' they are forever telling us to believe in.

As has been said elsewhere, the main political parties in this country - Conservative, Liberal Democratic, Labour - are middle class parties. So it's no accident that all but a handful of members of parliament are middle class. The allusion - the lie! - of 'free democratic elections' is one of the important ways that enables that to remain the dominate class. The squabbles between these parties are never about whether their class should be the dominate one, but they are always about how best to ensure that it remains so.

The vast majority of middle class people - from the 'top ranks' down to those such as teachers - want the present system of running things to stay broadly as it is. Yes, they to have disagreements among themselves about things like teachers pay, student grants, where airports - nuclear power stations should be built, nuclear waste dumps, nuclear disarmament, how big or small the crumbs should be that are thrown to the unemployed, and so on. They are wholly united in their opposition to any action which they think might be concerned with "the emancipation of the working class by the working class themselves, alone". For such action threatens their dominant position and the better life that they and their children will have from it.

Even the facade of 'democracy' is set aside when ever and wherever their power is - or they feel it to be - seriously threatened. Though in South Africa for example, the 'democratic' sham applies only (only ever has) to the white middle class. The great majority of the population, the black South Africans, are subjugated by a fascist like tyranny, a ruthless inhuman regime that would quickly collapse without the support of other middle classes of the world, particularly the British - a situation that will be dealt with in more detail later.

WHAT IS 'DEMOCRACY'?

Like the words 'socialism' and 'anarchism', the word 'democracy' is another which gets bandied around without ever being clearly defined by those who use it. There are people who seem to think that, although not knowing precisely what it means, it is nevertheless something, some condition, that is really useful and valuable to have. Well this vagueness is useful and valuable - to the dominant class! They use 'democracy' as a kind of cover-up for the true situation. They use it to describe and justify a system of government which ensures the continuation of their dominant ruling position.

An often heard and quoted definition of 'democracy' is that which has falsely been attributed as originating from Abraham Lincoln: 'Government of the people, by the people, for the people'. Speaking at Gettysburg in 1863 - where, in a battle of the American Civil War, 23,000 troops of the 'North' and 28,000 of the 'South' had been killed - Lincoln said: "We here resolve that these dead shall not have died in vain... and that government of the people, by the people, for the people, shall not perish from the earth".

But another American, Daniel Webster - one-time Secretary of State - had said something very similar 33 years earlier (1830); and 1700 years before that, Tacitus, the Roman historian, said it. Or go back a few hundred years BC and the Greeks were saying something very much the same. In fact, the word 'democracy' comes from two Greek words: 'demos' meaning 'people', and 'krateo' meaning 'rule'. The Greeks first used a form of government which they called 'democracy' in their small 'city-states' several hundred years BC where, in theory, every citizen could take part in decision making. But in reality, all the important decisions were made by the privileged 'noble' class, ie. the richest people, those who actually held political, military and religious power. These were the 'people' who 'ruled'; and all of them were men! Women were totally excluded. So were the slaves. Yet both Roman and Greek 'civilisations' were based on the thousands of slaves who did all the productive work - all the hard graft.

SO WHO ARE 'THE PEOPLE'?

It is surely obvious that 'government of the people, by the people, for the people' is, in a class divided society, totally impossible unless - unless 'the people' are the dominant class.

So that's one reason why, today, middle class governments justify their actions by saying that they were 'democratically' elected, implying that a majority of the electorate ('electorate' meaning all those entitled to vote every 4 or 5 years) actually voted for them. Yet this present government was voted for by only a minority of the electorate - and that's despite all the millions of pounds spent on electioneering, and all the heavy TV/radio/press propaganda.

It's surely obvious too that 'democratic' general elections are nothing more than the times when we are given the 'choice' of being governed by the middle class, the middle class, or the middle class.

But there's no 'democratic' cover-up in many other things - in management in industry for example. Here the managers themselves simply appoint any new members of the management, and the

workers don't get any choice at all about what sort of middle class person is to manage them - and, of course, they are not allowed to take part in any way that matters in the management's decisions.

'Half a century of social democracy'

George Grosz 1923

WHOSE LAW AND ORDER?

Here in Britain, even the screen of 'democracy' is becoming threadbare in places, and we are more often getting glimpses of what lies behind it. We got some in the 1984-85 miners strike when, for example, the ruthless and unprovoked violence of the police shocked even a few middle class liberals; also when they stopped miners in Kent from leaving their area and, under threat of arrest, made them go back home. 'It's a free country' - provided you do as you're told.

To keep their 'democratic way of life' they are continually having to increase the powers of the police - even licence to kill. In recent years we have seen several people, including Jimmy Kelly, Liddle Towers and Barry Prosser killed while in police custody. All this is happening despite whimpering squeaks of protest from middle class liberals like those in the National Council for Civil Liberties. Where they really stand was made clear by their General Secretary, Patricia Hewitt,* in July 1981 when, in reference to the 'riots', she said: "It is appalling that our police officers should now be facing petrol bombs".

> * Such attitudes and statements of Patricia Hewitt have shown her middle class 'comrades' that she's got the 'right' approach and knows which side her bread is buttered. This has enable her to climb up the jobs hierarchy a bit. She is now Neil Kinnock's press secretary, and is still getting it 'right'. In a letter published by 'The Sun' on 6 March 1987, she attacked 'the loony Labour Left' for supporting gays and lesbians (one of the better things they've done), adding that, if not stopped, it would cost Labour the election.

We are moving towards a point were they will believe that their 'democracy' might no longer ensure for certain their dominant position - they will then dispense with it. Since the beginning of the 70s, there has been an obvious transition towards a much more authoritarian society - and it will continue to get tougher. Its gradualness here is due to the continuing resistance - despite all the defeats - of British working class people. Though in some countries, where the resistance is weaker and the working class is more divided, the dominant classes may find it necessary and easier to impose a more open form of fascist totalitarianism.

As was indicated earlier, the middle class believe that 'a good and orderly society' depends on them remaining the dominant class - and hence the reason why 'law and order' is at or near the top of their agenda whatever the political party It is, of course, their kind of law and kind of order, for it is they alone who make the laws.

When they talk of 'law and order', they don't so much mean the laws governing, say, the sale of food and drink, or the control of traffic; they mean more the laws which deal, for example, with the various kinds of 'theft', for these 'crimes' affect their class a great deal more than they do working class people. But their main concern is laws which deal with anything they believe is, or could be, a threat to their class's dominant position. Some such laws, made centuries ago, they have retained, e.g. laws made to deal with the Peasant's Revolt in 1381 are still used today when it suits them; some have been reviewed, changed and added to; others have been more recently made, e.g.. anti-working class solidarity laws, like the one to stop you going to help your mates on strike; so-called 'secondary picketing'

LEGITIMATE MIDDLE CLASS CRIME

Those screaming about 'law and order' are not bothered about the middle class theft of million of pounds every year at the Stock Exchange, Lloyds, and the banks, which to date amounts to billions of pounds - none of it recovered. In fact, nobody knows - not even the police, the government, or the Attorney General - how much is stolen through 'City Crime' as it's called, other than that the amount is astronomical. Yet how often do you hear or read about it, let alone anybody being caught?

There was a little muted squeak about it on BBC-TV's Panorama programme on 4 November 1985 where it was said that since the police had 'failed' to do anything about 'City Crime' (hadn't seriously tried!), "the government now proposes that the financiers should police themselves." Like the fiddle of the police themselves investigating complaints against themselves, this was a certain recipe for even bigger swindles and thefts.

It was reported in the 'News' on 18 December 1986, that high-ranking civil servants (ie. the government's own middle class staff) are themselves making big profits on share-dealing by using 'inside information' - information which is supposed to be 'top secret' - and investigations are under way. But in fact, no action has been taken. Then there's the furor about take-over frauds - e.g. massive multi-million-pound fiddles by top middle class people in firms like Guinness. But still nobody's in nick for any of these crimes.

It's no accident that well over 90% of those in prisons are working class people. Most are inside for 'theft' of one sort or another, though the amounts in relation to middle class grand-scale thefts in the City alone, are minute - even in total.*

> *** IMPRISONED FOR PEANUTS**
> On 20 November 1986, the West Briton and Cornwall Gazette reported that three working class 'youths' aged 17, 18 and 19, had each got four months imprisonment for "joint charges of taking a Land Rover from Porthtowan without consent; stealing pears from Liptons in Redruth; entering the Penventon Hotel at Redruth as trespassers and stealing an ashtray; stealing a quantity of nails owned by Lark Construction Ltd." It wasn't said in Court how many, or what sort of nails, so perhaps they were the bosses toenails. However, it was said in Court of one of the three that "his saving grace is that he is in full-time employment." Christ knows what sentence he'd have got if he'd been unemployed.

THE REAL POLITICAL PRISONERS

But to paraphrase the much-used words of Richard Lovelace: 'Stone walls alone do not a prison make. Nor iron bars a cage', for the working class throughout the world are imprisoned. They are the real political prisoners, not the Solzhenitsins, the Sakharovs, the Shcharanskys, about whom the Western middle classes shed crocodile tears with such extravagant and hypocritical zeal. And even though the aim (as has been said) is to keep working class people in a state of permanent submission without the open use of force, this has by no means completely achieved, and in recent years we have seen the middle class 'authorities' use more obvious and organised violence - against workers in the coal-mining industries being one of the more visible examples.

In 1984-85, a terrific struggle was put up by the majority of men, women and children in the mining community, despite being manipulated into it at the wrong time by the union leadership, despite allowing this leadership basically to determine the methods and strategy of the fight, thus contributing to the eventual defeat, and despite the fact that the police exposed themselves as a para-military force - like those in other more obvious police-states - whose clear objective was to violently crush all effective resistance in the mining communities.

But at least equally important recent examples of organised violence, were seen at Bristol in 1980, Brixton, Toxteth, Handsworth, in 1981; Handsworth again and Tottenham, in 1985. And the importance of these 'insurrectionary outbursts', as some lefty intellectuals preferred to call them, is far greater than many of these intellectuals would have us believe. So let's look again at events the importance of which the media tried to diminish by calling them 'riots'.

Photo courtesy of Flint Michigan Underground Services

A HOPE BEYOND THE SHADOW OF A DREAM

During the ten days of July 1981 that shook the world's middle classes, '...this sceptered isle... this precious stone set in a silver sea... this blessed plot, this earth, this realm, this England...' (as we were taught in school) was severely shaken by outbursts of anger - and joy! - from working class people that had not been seen for many decades, and they engendered in many people 'a hope beyond the shadow of a dream.'

Parts of every major city in the land were rocked and rolled - as well as some of the most unlikeliest of towns. The media called these uprisings 'riots'. A riot is defined as 'debauchery, loose living, an outbreak of wanton behaviour,' and so on; hence the term 'riot' has, they believe, not only a more criminal implication, but also shows the 'respectable law-abiding' middle class's contempt for the interfering working class.

The uprisings began in various parts of London, particularly Brixton, and quickly spread to other big midland and northern cities such as Bristol, Birmingham, Derby, Manchester, Sheffield, Liverpool, and surprisingly, towns such as Cirencester, Market Harborough, Dunstable, Harlow, as well as middle class havens such as Knaresborough and Southport. The shocked middle class manipulators of the media, totally taken by surprise, at first gave these 'insurrectionary outbursts' sensational coverage - rather as a reflex action - until ordered by the government and police to hit it on the head. Consequently, the large number of places affected, and the extent and character of the fury, were not at any time reported. Though at a later date, Chief Constable Oxford let a kitten out of the bag when he said that 'few people realised just how close the police had been to completely losing the battle of Liverpool.'

The social and political importance of the uprisings was played right down. One way in which this was done was by the continually repeated announcement that the reason why they spread all over the country at such lightening speed was only because bored youngsters had seen reports of Brixton on TV, and had decided to have a bash too - the so-called copy-cat effect.

This was merely nervous wishful-thinking, for it was rarely the case. It's a fact that, since some time in the 70s, young people have been watching far less TV than they did during the years of it becoming a mass consumer item. According to the Daily Telegraph, both the BBC and the commercial TV companies, from top management downwards, are deeply worried about this 'phenomenon'. Obviously, these TV managers fear there is something more dangerous than the possibility of being made redundant.

The real reason is that young working class people have a much more efficient grapevine, around which news quickly travels, than the 'authorities' want to openly admit - although some police spokesmen did concede that it was 'very effective'. Incidentally, TV as a propaganda machine is not as powerful and effective in getting us to believe their lies as they think. Nor does it dominate our minds to the extent that many of the middle class theorists of the Left think - for their general underestimation of us blinds them to the fact that working class people can and do see through it, even if only at the times when it's most important to do so (see reference later to the BBC-TV's 'Six O'Clock News').

The majority of people who found joy in their anger that week were young, yet there were several cases where, when the grandchildren had opened up the joints, the grandparents got in on the free shopping. In Bristol, for example, a paraplegic 'senior citizen' was wheeled into a supermarket so's he could liberate a few things for himself.

In the English cities, young black people (mainly Afro-Caribbeans) played the principal roles, but in the sense that they opened up the gaps through which Asians and whites followed and, in many cases joined them. In Derby, mainly white young people who were 'insurrecting' in the smart city centre were driven by the police into the ghetto area of Normanton Road and Peartree. No doubt the aim of the police was to disrupt class unity, but it didn't work, for the place became a battlefield where most of the blacks, whites and Asians joined together to fight the police.

RACE RIOTS?

Initially, party politicians and the media said the uprisings were racial in character, but soon had to abandon that line as the truth began to force its way through the lies. Uprisings in Scotland and Wales, though not on the same scale as in England were hardly reported at all. Yet 'riotous assembly' in Glasgow made the usual Saturday-night aggro seem like a Tory Party conference in Bournmouth. Of course the original reason for suppressing 'riot' news from these two countries was that, as many people know, there are virtually no blacks there - a fact that immediately would have thrown their 'racial riots' lie into doubt, at least.

The press in Europe also initially reported them as racial, only to change their tune a couple of days later. The American press said the same in their first reports. Then, led by the New York Times, they actually emphasised class as 'the prime factor'. Several reports here confirmed this. For example, on 10 July 1981, the Guardian quoted an 'unemployed cockney skinhead' who, referring to the middle class said: "They're terrified of the blacks and whites rising together and storming the suburbs. That's where they ought to riot, in Finchley and Richmond". So, in July 1981, much of the media and many politicians eventually had to openly admit that 'the riots were basically non-racial'.

Nevertheless, media reporting still continued (still does) making racist insinuations, like calling all black people 'immigrants' though knowing that almost all young blacks were born here and that in some districts, such as Liverpool 8, a fair sized black community has existed for over a hundred years.

When they blamed racism among the working class as a cause of the uprisings, it was also a means of trying to console one another in the face of the frightening reality of their class nature. This is only one of the reasons why the middle class will continue to incite and encourage racism among working class people. Some of the ways they use are subtle, cunning and devious; others are open, dirty and crude like those used by newspapers such as the Sun, Mail and Telegraph - but all are obscene. And it's all part of the long-used strategy of 'divide and rule'.

Handsworth

EDITORS NOTE: more police funerals

ENEMIES RECOGNISED

Mass unemployment was also initially bandied around as a major reason for the uprisings. But this too was played down when it became known that large numbers of children were involved. In Manchester, for instance, an 8-year-old was arrested for setting fire to a bicycle shop; and out of 67 arrested on Park Road, Liverpool, 21 were 'juveniles' between the ages of 8 and 16.

The point was stressed by a Tory cabinet minister, William Whitelaw, who said: "Many of the hooligans were aged between 10 and 11, even less, so there can be no question of unemployment being the cause". The real point is that the kids knew - even if some only intuitively - that there was no future for them in terms of what used to be.

They knew (know!) too that the 'advice' of the so-called revolutionary left - dominated as it is by white middle class clever-dicks - was (is!) nothing more than a means of getting control over them for their own ends. Despite their anti-capitalist rhetoric, these 'revolutionary' groups and parties do not want to end the domination of the middle class, do not want working people to emancipate themselves - alone. They present no alternative to how society basically is run. On the contrary, their structure and organisation is a fairly accurate reflection of it. For instance, at the time of the uprisings, the International Marxists, the Socialist Workers' Party, The Workers' Revolutionary Party, through their papers Socialist Challenge, Socialist Worker, and Newsline respectively condemned all looting as 'unsocialist' and 'acts of vandalism by gullible youth'. No wonder nobody knows what 'socialist' means.

Hitler and his thugs called themselves 'class 'socialists'; paragons of middle class virtue like Roy Hattersley, Neil Kinnock, and the rest all say they are 'socialists'; Vanessa Redgrave, star of bourgeois stage and screen, and the Workers Revolutionary Party, says she is a 'socialist'. In fact, there are so many varieties of 'socialists' that the term is quite meaningless - worse than that, for there's already too much confusion without adding to it by joining in the endless competition for 'correct' definitions.

Media personnel are almost all middle class 'professionals' who - no matter how 'liberal' they appear to be - know exactly which side their bread's buttered. Many young people know this too, without having read a page of the reams of theoretical articles and analyses oozing from the middle class left. There were many cases where the 'professionals' of TV and press had the shit scared out of them - some actually coming under fire. In Brixton, for example, photographers from the Daily Star came under heavy attack, and ITN film vans were burnt out. A journalist from the Guardian (a paper as strongly pro-middle-class domination as any of the others, and often to be found soaking up the guilty sweat under the arm of your middle class liberal) got a good belting in Toxteth.

Nevertheless, some people were less aware of who their class enemy is and allowed infiltration by media mercenaries, only later to regret it when arrested after being identified from photographs and/or film of the action which media people had eagerly handed over to the police. Mind you, the police may not have needed such devoted assistance, for they were, in any case, taping TV newscasts on their own video-recorders.

And many more young working class people learnt - in addition to those who already knew - that teachers are their enemies. The Times stated that 'in Toxteth during the weekend riots, teachers had reported children they had seen, not only from their own schools in Liverpool, but also those from schools outside the city'. Another case in point was that, following the exceptionally furious uprisings in October 1985 which centered in and around the Broadwater Farm Estate in Tottenham, teachers invited the police into their classrooms to pick out children they alleged were involved,

For some years now, and in all kinds of ways, young working class people, both black and white, have been getting first-hand experience of who - what sort of people - are their real enemies. They've been getting it from violent police harassment on the streets and in their homes; from the domineering, self righteous attitudes and actions of local authorities (including educational psychologists, social workers, welfare officers, and the like), dole officers, DHSS officials and their snoopers, right up to the middle class 'leaders' of the ethnic groups.

They've also had other kinds of experience, like the slimy veneer of concern shown by idiotic hypocrites among party politicians and government ministers, who spent the odd hour talking to people in the 'trouble spots', 'ascertaining the facts' - facts which even if they were able to 'ascertain', they wouldn't comprehend. An ex-housing minister 'ascertaining' in Newcastle almost freaked out a young low-paid bus-driver when he asked, "but you do own your own bus don't you?"

Mind you, some of them know only too well what the 'facts' are, and while not exactly shitting themselves, are putting on plastic knickers just in case. How else can you account for their paranoia in the way they put down the miners in 1984-85? Yet the intensity of feeling in the Handsworth and Tottenham uprisings of September/October '85, showed that young working class people - and a significant number of older ones - were far from cowed by the spectacle only a few months earlier, of 10,000 police, some armed with weapons a lot more violent than batons, storming round the country in convoys, and acting as a paramilitary force to ferociously smash up the cars of miners and pickets, and battering the totally unarmed occupants, as well as their many vicious attacks on miners at pit-head gatherings, in their homes and in their streets.

Handsworth

POLICE CONTROL IN HANDSWORTH AND TOTTENHAM

Over 40% of people in Handsworth are unemployed, and over half the young people who've left school have never been employed. An attempt was made to partly patch up the very run-down area by a grant which enabled the police to be involved, particularly in the Lozells Road Project - a scheme which included an expensive youth centre. Soon, the police were employing heavy harassment tactics against the many 'youths' who didn't want to use the centre - for these 'youths' knew that it was mainly a means for the police to spy on them.

Despite the dilapidated state of the Broadwater Farm Estate in Tottenham, black people had made a bearable life for themselves and the white residents. They'd built up, and were themselves efficiently running, a youth centre, a play group, and a club for elderly people, black and white. All had been planned so that it could not be invaded by the police. But, just as with the Lozells Road Project, the police can't stomach it when black people show that they can rung things far better without police 'help', ie. without their approval and control. They'd invaded the estate many times in the previous few years - in November 1982, a riot squad occupied it without good reason for over two days.

Note: "A police cadet says that, of 26 recruits in his class, 19 had to have National Front tattoos removed." Management Today, January 1986.

THE ASIAN REVOLT

The 'Revolt of Islam' may well still be going on, but here among young Asians, it's more the revolt against Islam. These once submissive children (the Arabic word 'Islam' means 'submission') are breaking away from the stranglehold of the laws and practices of Muslims, as well as from those of Hindus and Sikhs. Most Asian community 'leaders' are store and restaurant owners, landlords, supermarket managers, etc., and it's an encouraging sign of growing working class consciousness that the appeals of these middle class 'leaders' to be peaceful and law-abiding in the face of oppression, are being ignored by young Asians.

A substantial part of the reason for this is that young blacks are being influenced by young whites whose respect for the bourgeois idea of family is now at an all time low. So the instilled artificial racial barriers are breaking down as young people are seeing more clearly that they have much more in common to unite about than there is to be divided over. But the struggle of young Asians is tougher, for they have additionally to fight against a much more reactionary family set-up; and a less-subtly, much more obviously, male-dominated 'culture' than that of the whites, with its chaperoned girls, arranged marriages, wives behind locked doors, and so on.

That they are nevertheless coming to grips with the problems was even confirmed by that creepy 'liberal', Mr Raj Nayan - a senior official of the Council for Community Relations in Leicester - when he said : "I think we're seeing an embryonic movement of poor working class white kids teaming up with similar black kids" (Daily Telegraph, 15 July 1981).

It's also a harder struggle for young Afro-Caribbeans, many of whose parents have a puritanical Victorian attitude and are very domineering. It is an attitude imposed on them back in the 1800s by middle class hypocrites calling themselves 'missionaries' who - as in Africa - went out to the West Indies with a Bible in one hand and a gun in the other. Part of an article in the Jamaican Gleaner' summed it up: "The facts about slavery and the obvious ways in which blacks were kept down are well known. But what is not so generally appreciated is the way in which we are colonised in our minds".

'The facts about slavery' (and the 'missionaries') are not as well known here in this country as this statement suggests, which is part of the reason why the subjects have been dealt with in much more detail below in the section on Africa.

A fair-sized number of black parents still preach, praise, and try to impose, principles about family, discipline and morals which over generations, white working class parents here have been pressured to comply with by middle class governments, magistrates, judges, clergy of all sorts, and other moral-hucksters. Some of these parents did as they were told - some still do. But this particular method of psychological control has been breaking down here since the disappearance of Victoria and Empire. And this breakdown continues despite would-be Victorian revivalists like those in the Thatcher government and elsewhere, who think that it used to work well for them, and are desperate today to get a tighter grip on a working class which they fear may now be on the road to rebellion.

BLACK CHILDREN REBELLING

So regardless of the apparently still-persisting legacy of 19th Century colonialism among black parents, their children - influenced as they may well be by whites - are rebelling against it. Examples of this are their refusal to stay at home in the evenings, to got to church, to lead a 'Christian life' - namely, to do nothing to change your lot, rely on a non-existent god, and look forward to a non-existent heaven - their refusal to obey orders forbidding dreadlocks, orders forbidding teenage sons and daughters from having friends of the opposite sex, and so on. As a result, many run away from home, and some are thrown out by their parents for their defiance and refusal to conform (perhaps it's an indication of the ratio between black and white family breakdowns that, during its first year in the late 70s, a hostel for homeless children at Waltham Forest catered for 64 black children and 11 white). Thus, another middle class whine, that the uprisings were due to lax, permissive working class parents and the break-up of the family, got it wrong again - or was it just wishful thinking? Maybe it was purposeful propaganda? Anyway, many family break-ups are due to the very opposite of 'lax' parents.

It has also been said that, due to mass unemployment, 'the family' is making a comeback - that one of the important control-methods of the German fascists in the 1930s of strengthening 'the family' by conditioning women to be almost solely concerned with 'Kinder, Küche, Kirche' (a Nazi slogan meaning Children, Kitchen, Church), is now being achieved here to some degree through unemployment causing many more women to be housebound. But so are many more men, and school-leavers. In fact, the pressures of unemployment tie everyone more to the home, which then becomes as tense and stressful as an over-crowded prison cell. This is not restoring the family unit, but straining it to breaking point. So the revival of the Happy Families game hoped for by all the fascist-minded members of the middle class, doesn't seem to have much chance.

THE SILLY 'TIMES'

Middle class children in the comfortable middle class homes - where generally there is much more room, privacy, more things to do, etc. - have fare fewer and far less intolerable things to rebel against, so a degree of 'laxity' among their parents is thought to be OK. The Times, pushing this 'permissiveness' line, was naively frank about it. An article published during the uprisings (11 July 1981), entitled "Why So Many Children Take To The Streets", summed up the reasons like this: "Permissiveness in child rearing during the past 10 years or so, while perhaps all well and good for the educated middle class in leafy suburbs, is counter-productive for families of manual workers living in inner-city housing estates".

'Permissiveness' in working class families the cause of uprisings? Or is this simply a lie the middle class cuddle up to in an attempt to comfort themselves? If it was written by some idiot with a sociology degree then perhaps it would be understandable why s/he has no fucking idea what's going on between working class parents - still, in varying degrees, influenced by bourgeois-imposed ideas about the right way to bring up children - and their totally pissed-off offspring.

But the middle class are not all as daft as the Times article suggests. If this situation appears at some point to be a serious threat to the well-being of their class, they will certainly have to do something about it. But what? They'll squabble about whether it's best to attempt to batter working class children into being more submissive, or whether the craftier more cunning approach of the 'liberal' sociologist would do the trick. Either way, they've got a big problem.

It would even cost far more than the £18,000 million spent each year on worse than useless armaments (useless to us that is, for without it their whole economy would collapse) to overcome the housing 'problem' alone - a 'problem' which virtually only affects working class people, millions of whom are either completely homeless and/or living in relatively atrocious conditions - never mind about the 'problem' of many frustrated young people who see no future for themselves in a crazy world where every day they are bombarded with advertising propaganda to buy, buy, buy with no, no, no money.

The good¬
the bad¬
and the
disgusting

THE HOUSING 'PROBLEM' THEY WON'T SOLVE

Today, there are many thousands more working class people homeless, and thousands more living in squalid conditions, than there were 22 years ago (1965) when the King Hill Campaign in Kent forced the plight of homeless families many times onto TV-screens and the front pages of almost every national newspaper. Even 'Shelter' the middle class do-gooding organisation, says that there are now 20 times more homeless than at that time. The middle class refer to this mass of human suffering as a 'problem'. They prefer this term to describe it because a 'problem' is 'a question proposed for solution', in other words, it holds out the hope of solution - that it can be solved. It can be! But the middle class won't do it.

Contemporary housing in Birmingham

Sure, middle class 'liberals' will deplore the situation, call it a 'scandal' and so on. But, as they said in a BBC2 'Open Space' programme on 9 October 1986, they "are powerless to stem the rising tide of homelessness". The programme drew attention to the fact that, under an Act about housing, local authorities are responsible for finding some sort of accommodation for homeless families in their areas, and that many could only do so by paying the cost of bed-and-breakfast in one room of a hotel. This meant, they said, that in "thousands of homeless families, parents and children alike are suffering months, even years, in cramped, unhealthy, and often dangerous, conditions". One homeless woman who appeared on the programme, said: "You're in prison and you don't know when your time's up".

BIG PROFITS OUT OF HOMELESSNESS

London's inner-city councils alone will this year pay out more than £40 million to middle class hotel owners for these hovel-like conditions, some of whom actually admitted on the programme that they were only in the business to make a profit, so no-one could blame them.

Of course, local authorities are 'powerless' to change this situation. If you've ever had to go to them, you'll know the middle class wallys who are being well paid for 'dealing' with the 'problem'; you'll know that they're just like those at the DHSS; you'll have felt the prying, arrogant, bossy attitude of many of them, and the pious, patronizing concern shown by the few others.

There are several reasons why housing for working class people is so appalling. At the same time as heavy expenditure on things like armaments and 'law and order' is increasing, heavy cuts have been made in house-building and maintenance. The working class has always been under attack by the middle class, but today it is more obvious. Many aspects of it can be seen, and housing in working class areas throughout the country is one. It can be seen particularly in the decline, decay, and dereliction of the inner-cities.

An official report on housing (5 March 1986) states that '85% of council housing is in a bad state of repair', and that 'it would cost £20,000 million to put things right'.

There are well over a million people 'qualified' to spend a long time on housing waiting lists; and there are many thousands of homeless people who are not 'qualified' (what sort of people decide who is and who is not 'qualified'...? You've guessed it). Yet at the same time, there are well over 100,000 good, fair-sized, habitable houses standing empty - many of them for years - which would accommodate hundreds of thousands of homeless people.

"In the inner London borough of Hackney, 15,000 families are on the housing waiting list. In Liverpool, there are 22,000. In Manchester, the sum needed for housing rehabilitation is £600 million. This is 3 times the amount shared out (late 1985) among **all** local authorities in England from what they got out of council house sales" (Management Today, January 1986).

THE PURPOSE OF COUNCIL HOUSE SALES

This is yet another reason for 'the housing crisis', as some of them like to call it - the heavy pressure applied through the corrupt 'buy-your-own-council-house' campaign. And some working class people have fallen for it - they wouldn't be members of a dominated class if they hadn't.

Council house selling not only has the obvious effect of making things worse for poorer people by reducing the number of houses to let, but it also has the less obvious political objectives. For instance, working class people with the halter of mortgage repayments around their necks are less likely to cause trouble (through strikes, etc.) and will, they hope, see themselves less as members of the dominated class. Also, on council estates, divisions are created between those who are buying and those who can't - a constant objective of the dominant class.

Housing for working class people was never very good, and quite often very bad - badly designed, badly built, and badly maintained. All housing was/is designed by middle class architects for handsome remuneration, and built by middle class owned firms for handsome profits. And when faults appear, as they often have in the ghastly boring blocks of flats for example, when they have gradually disintegrated or collapsed, those responsible have not been given the flaming necklace, or even just a knee-capping - they've simply not been looked for.

THE REASONS FOR 'THE WELFARE STATE'

For many working class people things are getting worse. No real economic pundit can predict a significant reduction in numbers of people unemployed. A couple of years ago, the Cambridge Econometrics Unit came up with an obviously tongue-in-cheek prediction that unemployment will only begin to fall in the year 2000, but couldn't even base this 'optimism' on any faintly credible assumption as to how and why this might come about. In fact 'realistic' economists can only predict a continuing increase. There are, as was shown above, some 29 million working class people living around or below the 'official' poverty line. Their main 'assistance' - through two Departments of the 'Welfare State' - comes from Unemployment Benefit, Supplementary Benefit, and the Health Service, which continues to be cut by the Conservatives. Many of their class in the other parties, especially Labour, see the dangers of this. The reason why they think these cuts are dangerous goes back to the reason why such 'welfare services' were set up in the first place.

The National Insurance Act of 1911 was brought in by the most powerful middle class party of the time - the Liberal Party under the leadership of Herbert Henry Asquith, first earl of Oxford and Asquith - as a 'concession' to the working class. This was one of the first indications of how middle class politicians were thinking during a period of considerable and increasing working class militancy, particularly from miners, dockers, seamen and railwaymen (In 1908, there were about 400 strikes; in 1913, there were 1,500, troops being used on several occasions to suppress them). This upsurge in working class anger was due to bad and worsening living conditions, and the failure of the Labour Party to show that it was either able or willing to do anything about it.

WORLD WAR I AND THE LABOUR 'PATRIOTS'

Then came World War I, and this had some effect in stemming the tide of workers' hostility due mainly to pressure put on them by the aggressive nationalism of flag-waving leaders of the Labour Party and trade unions who screamed for 'patriotic co-operation in the war-effort'. A particularly sick example of where they really stood was shown by the middle class Arthur Henderson, the first Labour MP to be a government minister in various war-time cabinets. As such, he put all his influence and energy into breaking strikes, and into suppressing working class opposition and resistance to the introduction of conscription in 1916.

This 'patriotism' - the last refuge of scoundrels, as it was once politely called - exposed their true class allegiance in a situation where millions of working class people suffered at home, and who fought, were maimed and killed in the most obscene conditions abroad, all in defence of, and on behalf of the middle class.

The suffering of working class people did not end with the war in 1918, for class-war continued and intensified - as it did throughout

Europe, due in no small way to the influence of the revolution in Russia. But here in this country it was the Labour Party which came to the rescue of the middle class by containing and restricting this fight-back - by still trading mainly on the illusion that it was a working class party.

THE GENERAL STRIKE

In 1925, the colliery owners announced their intention to drastically cut miners' wages and lengthen their working hours. Of course, the miners made it clear that they would fight against such action. The situation simmered on until April 1926. On May 1st, to force the miners into submission, the owners shut down the mines - in other words they locked the miners out. The TUC was pressed into calling a General Strike. It began on May 3rd, and immediately over 2 million workers came out on strike. The numbers were still growing - over 4 million out - when ten days later, on May 12th, the TUC leaders called it off. Why? The answer is simple. The middle class were shit scared.

A strong revolutionary mood was by then clearly developing among working class people, and control of the strike was quickly passing to them and out of the hands of those who ran the TUC and the Labour Party. Their 'cover' - as a party of and for the working class - was again blown, for in May 1926 the working class suffered possibly its worst defeat in history, a defeat which couldn't have been brought about without the decisive assistance of the Labour Party.

It was wrong to call them 'traitors', as some did. They were not 'traitors'. They were not guilty of disloyalty, of violating an allegiance to the working class. Their main loyalty and allegiance was to the middle class. So it was simply that, again, the middle class run Labour Party had come to the aid of the middle class, just as it did several times throughout the years of the so called 'depression' that followed.

Despite all this, large numbers of working class people were still not fully aware of the Labour Party's true nature.

THE TRUTH ABOUT LABOUR NOW BECOMING CLEARER

A political party for the working class run by middle class people is a contradiction that, over the years, has manifest itself as a dilemma of the Labour leaders - in other words, how to keep the Party's true nature and role disguised; how to keep alive an illusion.

Today, the dilemma seems to have been partly resolved, for the disguise has been dropped. Who runs the Labour Party, and who is likely to benefit most from it forming a government, is clearer now to more working class people, a significant number of whom just don't vote at elections.

But many still vote for the Labour Party - even though some with increasing cynicism and contempt - and the blame for the extent that they are still unaware of its true role can be placed squarely on the Left, and particularly on the various Trotskyist groupings. They still join in the election deception with stupid slogans such as 'Vote Labour Without Illusions'. They still rabbit on about making the Labour Party 'again' a party of the working class; that all that's needed is a change of leadership - into a leadership like those who lead their parties and groups - to make it 'again' something it never was.

However, middle class 'leaders' particularly politicians, were fully conscious of it. For example, in 1931, large cuts in working class living standards were being proposed so as to help the middle class with their financial problems - e.g. unemployment benefit was to be reduced by 20%, from 30 shillings to 24 shillings a week. A 'political crisis' developed causing King George V to call Stanley Baldwin (the ruthless Tory prime minister during the general strike, and later an ardent sympathiser of the fascist regimes in Germany and Italy) and Sir Herbert Samuel (Liberal leader, made a viscount in 1937) to Buckingham Palace for advice. By chance, Samuel arrived there first and got cracking on the 'advice-giving' straight away. He told the royal parasite that "in view of the fact that the necessary economies will prove most unpalatable to the working class, it will be to the general interest if they can be imposed by a Labour government." (Quoted from: Sir Harold Nicolson, 'King George The Fifth- His Life and Reign', Constable & Co. 1952, p.461)

In the event, a National Government was formed (26 August 1931) and several Labour 'stalwarts' joined it. Ramsey MacDonald - who had been prime minister in the former Labour government (1929), and who had so embarrassed some of his Labour Party colleagues by his undisguised obsession with the wealthy, the aristocracy and the royals, was made prime minister. Labour's middle class 'stalwart', Philip Snowden became Chancellor of the Exchequer and that evening, MacDonald, with a self satisfied look of joyful anticipation, said to Snowden: "Tomorrow, every Duchess in London will be wanting to kiss me." And kiss the bastard they no doubt did, for the squeeze on the working class was tightened as the economies necessary to the well-being of the middle class were imposed.

The US middle class, who had done so well out of the carnage of World War 1, thus enabling their economy to boom, panicked in October 1929 when the boom began to falter, and rushed to sell their shares. This caused the so-called Wall Street Crash and the near collapse of their economic system, Capitalism. The Crash had an equally disastrous affect on the economies of the middle classes in many other countries of the world, particularly Europe. In the years of 'depression' that followed, it was, as already pointed out, again the working classes who suffered most.

With so many millions of them unemployed (e.g. 13 million in the USA, near 4 million in the UK, 6 million in Germany) there was the misery and torture of grinding poverty as middle class governments 'imposed' on them 'the necessary economies'.

Ramsey MacDonald - Socialist

PREPARATION FOR WAR = ECONOMIC RECOVERY- AGAIN!

Economic recovery, greatly assisted by rearmament - i.e. preparation for war began in the USA and Europe in 1933 as fascist parties in Italy and Germany became more and more powerful. It should be noted that, at this time, the middle classes in these countries made up almost the entire membership of such parties which were enthusiastically supported by the owners and managements of most industries, as well as by the police and the armed forces. (see below: 'Middle Class Fascism' page 51)

Then came World War 2 and as before, it was the working classes who suffered most, so by the end in May 1945 there was a real and strong revolutionary mood amongst them throughout Europe. This the middle class leaders had to somehow dampen down, contain and restrain.

(How and why the working classes were restrained during the months following the end of the war, particularly by the Communist party government in the USSR and those of its dependent countries in Eastern Europe, but also by the governments in the West, is described more fully in the book 'Hungary 56', chapters titled 'East-West Agreement' and 'Liberation?'. Some copies of the U.S. edition still available in this country.)

LABOUR TO THE RESCUE - AGAIN!

Here in Britain, it was the Labour Party that was able to do the 'restraining'. This was made more easy for them because (as has been said) working class people still basically believed the lie fostered by one of the dominant class' most important allies, the middle class left, that Labour was a 'socialist' party concerned with their well-being.

On the wave of working class hunger for fundamental change, Labour gained a landslide victory in the general election of July 1945 and Clement Attlee who for the previous five years had been showing his class loyalty as deputy to Churchill, became prime minister.

The new Labour government's so called 'programme of austerity' was nothing more than a set of measures designed to help re-establish profitable accumulation. Among these measures was the bringing under State-ownership (i.e. nationalization) of industries that were 'failing', such as coal, steel, transport, gas and electricity. For many workers in these industries, things got worse. Private owners (richly compensated!) may have gone, but the same bosses remained and often became more ruthless.

This national reconstruction of the middle class' economic system, capitalism, again meant frustration, poverty and misery for many working class people. The Labour party's promises and several of the working class' hard-fought-for rights, went by the board. The Labour government, which had introduced a 'wage freeze' in 1948, dealt harshly with working class resistance. After declaring 'states of emergency' under the Emergency Powers Act of 1920, they sent in troops to break up numerous strikes and scores of militant strikers were imprisoned - for these 'socialists' had kept intact clause 1305 of an Act of Parliament, agreed by Churchill and Attlee in 1940, which made all strikes illegal: an act that was still in force when the Tories took over in 1951.

A 'WELFARE STATE' IS ONLY NECESSARY IN A CLASS DIVIDED SOCIETY

It was in the atmosphere of working class resistance that a more comprehensive health and social security system was set up. Based on a report by Lord Beveridge* in 1942, it was now embraced and acted upon by the Labour government.

* BEVERIDGE A LEADING ENEMY
William Henry Beveridge (1879-1963): Chief civil servant involved in the social legislation of Lloyd George's government; Director of Labour Exchanges 1906-1916; Director of the London school of Economics until 1937, then became Master of University College Oxford; Chairman of the Committee on Social Insurance which in 1942 issued the report mentioned above and which, incidentally, strongly advocated that an unemployed person must take any job which the authorities decided s/he could do, or lose state assistance. He became a Liberal MP for Berwick-upon-Tweed in 1944, lost his seat in the 1945 election, but was made a 'Lord' by the Labour government in 1946.

Beveridges ideas did not emerge from pure bourgeois do-goodism as some would have us believe, but were based on the reasonable (for them) conclusion that sometime in the near future, when the war was over, large sections of an angry and disgruntled working class would be further stirred up by having to suffer while the middle class clawed in the main 'benefits' of a massive reconstruction programme. It was concluded therefore that sops would have to be given to appease the working class and undermine their militancy. Also a 'better' health service would have the added advantage of, they thought, ensuring that healthier people would be better able to do the work necessary for this 'national reconstruction'.

It was not long, however, before sections of this 'Welfare State' began to be whittled away, until today even greater cuts are being made and others planned-for example, in Social Security as laid down in the Fowler Report. A significant number of the middle class, and not only the more fascist minded among them, feel that through the agency of a Tory government, they are now in a strong position to do this at a time when the working class-with five million of them unemployed, nearly nine million of them on very low pay and the most militant section, the miners, defeated - are demoralized and apparently unable to put up any affective resistance, let alone threaten attack.

THE AWFUL POSSIBILITY

Almost every middle class person, in some degree, fears working class potential to put an end to their dominant position. They glimpsed this 'awful possibility' in 1981/1984-85 through the anger and self-organizing ability of the mining communities in the face of the tremendous odds against them, as well as through the fury shown in the uprisings. But it's the deeper-thinking elements among them who do not go along with the Tory- type analysis that now is the time to settle the hash of the working class once and for all.

These elements of the middle class, of whom perhaps the largest number are to be found in the Labour Party, see such an approach to the 'problem' as a short sighted tactical mistake which underestimates working class strength, endurance, resilience, and ability to bounce back. These 'deeper thinkers' have noticed that working class people have been ground down many times before only each time to recover; If mistakes are made now, they argue, who knows what the next bounce back will lead to? To rely on the introduction of hundreds more police with more sophisticated equipment and using more para-military tactics, is too optimistic. Far better they think, to keep to a formula which up to now has worked. Part of that formula is in a Social Security system which allows a minimum standard of existence below which, they have calculated, it would be reasonable to expect people to rebel in sufficient numbers (joined by, say, the mining communities) as to pose a serious threat to the whole of their 'democratic society' and consequently, to their class' position in it.

The miners' strike and the uprisings were indications of 'the awful possibility'. Could they be the only indications they're likely to get without it actually happening?

A DILEMMA?

This 'formula', designed partly to sustain the dominance of our enemy the middle class, does of course suggest that we ought not to be fighting to preserve, defend and/or to improve it. But this is not quite the dilemma facing us that it at first appears. For we must bear in mind that the Labour Party, despite its 'deeper thinking' elements, has shown itself in the past to be quite prepared to cut into the 'Welfare State', has done so, and for reasons not unsimilar to those of the Tories. It is therefore a perfectly valid and progressive activity for working class people to fight against anything that attempts to make things worst for them, e.g. the cuts in unemployment and supplementary benefits. For one thing it can and sometimes does, force the enemy to keep changing strategy, which apart from making it more difficult for them, often exposes and weakens their tactics.

But among those campaigning to stop cuts, there are some who are supporting teachers' campaigns for more pay etc. Yet teachers make things worse for the working class. Helping them means helping those involved in conditioning, indoctrinating, disciplining and getting children to accept that the middle class are entitled to dominate us, are entitled to the best this society has to offer, are entitled to rule, because they are 'superior' - it means helping them, in effect, to get more pay for brainwashing our children!

EDUCATION?

Brainwashing is described as a technique of coercive persuasion used to alter a person's basic beliefs and attitudes without his/her consent. Such technique involves attempts to render a person's beliefs so 'useless' that 'new ones' are more easily substituted; at the same time, specific procedures (such as physical abuse and isolation) are designed to make the subject dependent on those doing the brainwashing and consequently, receptive to their ideas.

Through the middle class's media, we used to hear a lot about how they deplored such brainwashing techniques which they generally said were being used by Russia and other regimes in the East. Then we saw that agencies of the British middle class were using similar techniques (e.g. White Noise) in Northern Ireland and were eventually found guilty of it at the International Court of Justice in the Hague- since then, the media's kept it's gob shut on the subject.

But brainwashing of the working class - in a form closely related to the description given above, though the techniques are often more subtle and sophisticated, has been going on generation after generation, mainly through the state schools. As far as young children are concerned however, the techniques are less about altering a person's basic beliefs, for some may be too young to have any strongly held ones. But they are about implanting beliefs and attitudes designed to lead them to accept that the 'best' things done in the world have only been done by people of dominant classes - whether ancient Greeks, Romans, Royalty, Nobility or the middle class - and that today the middle class are 'superior' as is their way of running society.

Part of the brainwashing process, the most important part, is done by teachers through the Education System. It's a system staffed almost solely by middle class people; a system in which a section of them decide how working class pupils are to be disciplined and kept in line; a system in which they decide on the curriculum- what subjects, how they are to be taught and how much time is given to each; and it is they who decide how assessments, tests and exams are to be devised and carried out, the object of which is the acquisition of particular generalized standards.

The tendency today is clearly for even stricter control in their aim to keep working class children unaware of their position as a dominated class. The 'new' proposals put out in the name of Keith Joseph and later, Kenneth Baker, would appear to put the emphasis on what they call a 'record of achievement' whereby a child is followed through his/her schooling (and no doubt beyond!) by a 'record' showing every bit of information, every element, every detail - even details which at the time may be thought to be trivial - of the child's activities from the age of five. This 'record of achievement' device, which they say would be more useful to employers than exam results, makes the rotten exam system look quite liberal. It is also part of 'the tendency towards fascism in education' which is discussed further on.

A 'liberal' critic of the education system has recently lamented that "education is no longer concerned to be an extension and complement to the voluntary acquisition of knowledge through learning." Others have had similar moans. The point is that compulsory mass education never has been concerned to be that. Such whining wimps seem to know what's going on, but apparently have no idea why. Middle class 'educationalists' have constructed an education system which curbs, and in far too many cases kills a child's natural ability and eagerness to learn. They have sought with some degree of success, to construct a system that actively discourages working class people from thinking, other than very superficially, about how and why society is run the way it is - a system that in no way could lead them to conclusions about their position in society that would motivate a desire to effectively challenge the dominance of the middle class.

On the contrary the education system is intended to lead them in the opposite direction - into obedience, into deference and respect for their middle class 'superiors', into accepting their lot, into accepting that it's 'natural' for the dominant class, that it's 'right' that they should run the political parties, the government, all industries, the police, the courts, the prisons, the schools...

EQUAL OPPORTUNITY?

'Ah! But there is equal opportunity,' they'll whine. You'll even hear idiots of the Left say that's what they're striving for. You'll also hear 'equal opportunity' put forward as a goal by people you thought would know better. 'Equal opportunity' for what? Success? What is 'success'? 'Success' in this society is basically making more money than most other people. It's ludicrous pointing to 'self-made' toadying dingbats like Derek Jameson as a working class 'success'.

But by pushing the 'equal opportunity' line they hope to fog over the issue of class. It is a false proposition, an impossibility for a dominated class - just another of the middle class's much propagated lies. If one of two people in prison is chained hand and foot to the wall, you don't give them both 'equal opportunity', to escape by opening the prison gates.

Yet although there are a considerable number of working class people who are unaware that they are members of a dominated class, there is a number who are aware of it. This is a further indication that the middle class, despite all the facilities at their disposal, are not almighty, but are definitely vulnerable and can be defeated. That they know this is why they put so much effort into trying to prevent working class consciousness. 'Education' is a very important weapon to them in this objective. (There are of course others. For one, just look at how often we hear all this crap about management and managed having a 'common interest' that 'co-operation' is the way forward and so on.)

A FEARFUL SYSTEM

In most families, the job of moulding children to conform and obey 'authority' (i.e. that of the parents) is already well under way when, at five years old they are compelled by law to attend school. For, during this five years, many parents have been instilling in their children, middle class views and attitudes that have been systematically implanted in themselves over the years through their parents, school, the media and various other means. Then these children are taken over by the teachers in the state schools.

A few of them may have started what they love to call 'their careers' with the good intention of teaching children the truth about society, of giving them hope, perhaps bringing them joy - like Ursula, the heroine of D.H. Lawrence's novel 'The Rainbow'. She becomes a teacher (chapter 13) at the Brinsley Street School where "she would realize her dream of being the beloved teacher, bringing light and joy to her children." But to her horror, she soon discovers "the task of compelling the children into one disciplined, mechanical set, reducing the whole set to an automatic state of obedience and attention and then of commanding their acceptance of various pieces of knowledge."

Gradually, she becomes like the tyrannical and hated headmaster, Mr Harby: "..... she seized her cane and slashed the boy who was insolent to her, over head and ears and hands. And at length they were afraid of her, she had them in order... She who shrank from the thought of physical suffering in any form, had been forced to fight and beat with a cane and rouse all her instincts to hurt. And afterwards she had been forced to endure the sound of their blubbering and desolation when she had broken them to order."*

✱ WHY QUOTE LAWRENCE?

Lawrence was a coal-miner's son who got out of the pits and somehow got into Nottingham University, following which he took up a 'career' as a <u>teacher</u>. 'The Rainbow' got heavily attacked because it was anti-war (WW1) at a time when aggressive macho patriotism was at it's height - it also led to police prosecution for 'obscenity'. He eventually ran off to live with a married woman of the German aristocracy (von Richthofen), and they later got married. He was ill with tuberculosis for most of his life, and died from it at the age of 45.

Lawrence can be rightly despised for the fact that, quite early on in his life, it became clear that he was a screwed-up hater of women; and for the fact that (probably from the time he went to university) he was a toady of the middle class and their squalid 'values'. But what is quoted above from his novel, about how the education system brought any 'idealistic' middle class teachers to heel, is nonetheless true.

We can truthfully add that this Ursula was then faced with the choice facing any 'liberal-minded' teacher: either suppress and forget all good and altruistic intentions, or get out of the industry. 'The Rainbow' was published in 1914; today, fewer if any, go into the business with such illusions, for the techniques of modern Teacher Training Colleges soon put paid to such 'silly notions'. Even if any did somehow manage to get through still believing that schools should be run in a totally different way, a way that would bring 'light and joy' to working class children, a way that would expose more positively to them how they are an oppressed class, how that situation could be changed, and also then attempted to put this belief into practice, they would soon find themselves facing the frantic fury of the 'educational authorities'. These 'educationists' would charge them with crimes they themselves have always been guilty of, like 'rape of innocent children's minds' and so on, and such teachers would be out on their arses before you could say 'Secretary of State for Education and Science'.

For some time now, education in state schools has been a pre-packaged commodity, forcibly-fed to young consumers through a nationalized system of distribution, and where 'achievement' is measured by the degree to which the young consumers swallow, digest and regurgitate the package. It is a system based on fear.

UNDER THE CLASSROOM DOOR

TRICKLES A THIN STREAM OF BLOOD –

FOR HERE BEGINS THE MASSACRE OF THE INNOCENTS

a poem by
Miroslav Holub

The degree to which the teacher is not feared by the children, is the degree to which the children are feared by the teacher, or put another way - if the teacher doesn't fear the children, then the children fear the teacher and vice versa.

Fear is the only thing that makes the children call the teacher 'sir/miss', sit still, stand up when speaking or being spoken to by the teacher, not talk after the bell goes, do homework.... It's out of fear that they remain silent in the face of verbal attacks - the belittling sarcasm and ridicule they're subjected to when they've been unable to do something just how the teacher wanted. All this is intended to instill and reinforce in the minds of these future adults, the 'superiority' of the teacher, hence the 'superiority' of the middle class.

THE TENDENCY OF FASCISM

The tendency towards fascism in today's society is reflected in schooling, and vice versa - for fascism is not just the political doctrine of some other country, but a product of class divided society. Fascism is first and foremost a chronically disturbed emotional condition which is endemic and rooted in the dominant class* (though obviously it can and does spread to the dominated class), and which expresses itself in a variety of ways. It can be detected in the hierarchy of 'education': the government minister, the local council, the board of governors, the headmaster, deputy headmaster and so on, and among the children themselves where ranks are created like head prefect, monitor, top of the class, bottom of the class.... There is even a hierarchy of subjects e.g. maths, engineering, science, near the top and 'the arts' at the bottom. It can be seen in the rules and regulations aimed at 'discipline' and in the dull faces and sullen eyes of many children.

We can see fascism in the system of punishments - caning etc.- and in the way kids are compelled to rigidly stand in 'assembly'; in the meaningless religious ritual which still begins the day in many schools, where thousands of vivacious children have been bullied and cowed into reciting 'prayers' which to them are ridiculous and/or incomprehensible, to a god they either don't believe in, or fear, or hate - and then they have to chant some mournful, fucking boring hymn.

* FASCISM A MIDDLE CLASS DISEASE

In Italy, membership of the Fascist Party grew from a few hundred in 1919 to over 250,000 in 1921. Virtually all were middle class and included industrialists, landowners and the vast majority of police and army officers. The reason for this growth in membership was the middle class's fear of the increasing strength and militancy of the working class and the peasantry. It was due to this full backing of the middle class that Mussolini (who had previously been a school teacher!) was able in 1922, after a threatened coup, to take power.

The fascists' rise to power in Germany and Spain - though at different times and in different ways - was also due primarily to the full support and innate fascism of most sections of the middle classes in these countries: for there are no depths of inhumanity to which they will not sink to safeguard their dominant position when they believe it is threatened by the increasing frustration, anger and militancy of working class people.

The reasons are the same for the strength of the fascists at this period in countries as apparently diverse as Hungary, France, Finland and Norway.

I say, Ponsonby, tell those working class rotters to get out of our way

WHY MIDDLE CLASS CHILDREN DO 'BETTER'

As already said, the home conditions of middle class children are such that they have far fewer and far less intolerable things to rebel against than most working class children. This is also part of the reason why they appear to do much 'better' at school, pass more of the exams set by the exclusively middle class educationists. Yet we often hear middle class 'intellectuals' - 'libertarian revolutionaries' among them - lamenting this fact. Are they really that naive and ignorant?

Education is an institution which is essentially middle class, so these 'intellectuals' ought therefore to be able to see without too much effort that middle class children are favoured within schools - schools in which middle class 'values' are transmitted to middle class children whom teachers decide are 'brighter'.

Middle class children are not only favoured by teachers in the more strictly educational sense, but also in other ways, in behaviour for example. When a teacher's middle class little darlings are 'acting in a disorderly manner', the class as a whole is told off, whereas when the culprits are un-favoured working class children, they are picked out individually and denounced by name, quite often with sneering sarcasm and ridicule.

Another reason, and one connected with this favouring, is that middle class teachers don't expect working class children to be as 'good' and 'bright' as middle class ones. Experiments have been carried out in recent years 'proving' that if a child is treated as inferior and is not 'expected' to perform as well as the favoured child, then (regardless of his/her particular ability) s/he will perform and behave as 'expected', namely in an inferior way - and, as has been stressed elsewhere, they try to make working class people feel inferior throughout their lives. Of course children who more generally get the most shitty end of the stick are those who are black, working class and female.

We must continually bear in mind that the situation could not be otherwise, for if it were, we would not have a class-divided society. You can't have a society dominated by the middle class in which the education system is neutral, where the courts are neutral, the police are neutral...

THE INDUSTRY MANUFACTURING THE 'ELITE'

There is obviously nothing neutral about the expensive private schools, and no attempt is made whatever is made to disguise the fact. On the contrary, children in these swanky educational factories are clearly led to see themselves as 'superior' to the rest, therefore entitled to a better deal, to better jobs, entitled to respect from, and scornful of, the working class; they see themselves entitled to be arrogant, to boss others around, to become 'leaders' and in some cases, of their class - as indeed do many from the more notorious public schools, i.e. those of the so-called Headmasters Conference, where 'prestige' is as substantial as the fees.

CAN THE EDUCATION SYSTEM BE IMPROVED?

The answer to this question is an emphatic NO! Without totally-fundamental change in all aspects of this society - change for example that would make one element of education "an extension and complement to the voluntary acquisition of knowledge through learning" - no reformist tinkering by middle class 'liberals' could be an improvement. For they will undertake nothing that might lead to the elimination of their class's power over the working class.

As things are, the majority of the middle class, including some of the few 'liberals', believe that even tougher discipline is needed - they want to increase the fear level. They angrily tell us that teachers are sometimes assaulted by children: and there has been over the years, the odd report of such in the press. But how many times do we read of teachers' physical attacks on children? Yet this happens every day in every school! And there is not only physical violence; there is also assault by various psychological means, some of which have already been mentioned.

Clearly the government believe that cuts in education staff, facilities etc... will 'improve' the financial situation in their economic system as a whole; for if spending on arms (to take perhaps one of their most flagrantly insane priorities) is to continue at £8,000 million a year, cuts have to be made in other areas as well as in 'benefits' to the poor. In any case with unemployment remaining so high and probably increasing, a cut-back in the 'quality of production' at the education factories is seen, at least by the Thatcherite section of the middle class, simply as 'realistic economics'. It also has the added bonus of putting pressure on middle class parents in particular to send their children to private schools.

SUMMERHILL - AN IMPROVEMENT?

Despite all this, some silly 'liberals' point to the few private, fee-paying schools where there is considerably less 'discipline' than elsewhere, as a way of improving the system. Probably the best known of these is Summerhill, founded by A.S. Neill over 60 years ago. True, pupils here do have much more freedom than in state schools; for example, they can choose when and whether to go to a lesson on a particular subject or not - though there is no choice about what subjects are taught, which are virtually the same as in the other schools. And these subjects and the methods of teaching them are no less strongly coloured by the notion of middle class superiority, regardless of attempts to give it all a 'liberal' tint.

Summerhill is a school almost solely for the children of middle class parents able to pay the fees; so there is no need to differentiate between middle class and working class, no need to particularly favour the middle class kids and expect them to be 'better' and 'brighter' than the working class ones. The tiny minority of the latter who are admitted to the school are no more than a token - like your token blacks in films, TV, etc. They are tools used by a certain few middle class 'liberals' to ease their nagging feelings of guilt; they are like orphans in one bloody great middle class family - yet they are conditioned in much the same way as in the state schools. Although here - isolated, cut off from their working class friends and surroundings - they more easily get sucked into a sickly form of bourgeois liberalism. And despite the fight that some of them put up against it, over the years, a few went on to count among Neill's 'successes'.

These 'successes' were those he proudly directed attention to (as do his followers today) in defence of and in justification for his 'free' methods, namely, the high percentage of Summerhill pupils who had become 'captains of industry', army generals, heads of civil service departments, criminal court judges and so forth.

Summerhill, and the other handful like it, are 'educational mavericks', 'strays', schools that operate outside the main system; and while they remain such a minute minority, they can be tolerated, since they pose no threat whatever to the status quo. But there is not the faintest chance of such methods being introduced into the national education system while the middle class are in control; for they devised it, they run it and they know (even if in some of the thicker among them it's not much more than a subconscious reaction) that the system as it plays an extremely important part in maintaining their dominant position.

CHILDREN BEGINNING TO FIGHT BACK

There is however, encouraging evidence that children are beginning to fight back, not only at the violence of the education system, but also as they become more aware of the futility of a system geared partly to fit them into jobs that don't exist, followed by cons like those in the government's 'Action For Jobs'. There are more and more actions by school children which are either not reported at all, or are played down by the media. There are many examples, but here are just a few.

Although the burning of schools by children is not that uncommon, very little detail was given about the wave of school - burning that went on in Tyneside during the early 70's. On 23 February 1982, the Daily Telegraph briefly reported that at St. Saviours Church of England School in Toxteth, Liverpool, "pupils have wrecked classrooms by fire and vandalism and turned fire extinguishers on any teacher who dared to remonstrate." As to why they should do this, the Telegraph was dumbfounded.

> **SUNDAY SCHOOL - OF THEIR OWN FREE WILL!**
> "Children play truant all week and then go back on Sundays-of their own free will - to set fire to the schools. They're trying to tell teachers something."
> Management Today, January 1986.

We do know something about the many children who actually took part in the uprisings of 1981 and 1984-85. Yet little is known about the children in South Yorkshire, particularly in Doncaster and Sheffield, who at the beginning of 1985, went on strike and physically attacked their schools, first in support of the miners, then in solidarity with their schoolmates who were subsequently victimised. Here again other than the inevitable branding as 'vandals'* by the local middle class - controlled press, little else was said. Even bigger actions took place shortly afterwards in places as far apart as Bradford, Glasgow and Southampton. There were also many small -scale strikes on issues such as the compulsory wearing of uniforms.

BUILD A BONFIRE
BUILD A BONFIRE
PUT THE TEACHERS
ON THE TOP
PUT THE PREFECTS
IN THE MIDDLE
THEN WE'LL BURN
THE BLOODY LOT

LONG LIVE VANDALISM!

✱ The Vandals were Teutonic people said to be Asian Christians and haters of Roman Catholicism - who during the first 6 centuries A.D., roamed around Europe, particularly around the Mediterranean (they captured Rome for a time in 455), attacking and destroying Catholic churches where many of the things of value and much of the so-called art of the time was kept.

Hence, presumably, the dictionary definition of a modern vandal is: 'One who ignorantly destroys works of art and things of beauty.' If todays schools are 'things of beauty', long live vandalism!

Attacks on schools throughout the country occur quite frequently. Even in the political backwater of Cornwall, several reports have leaked out in recent years of schools being broken into, cases of cups and trophies being smashed up and other things being set on fire - but nothing was nicked. Presumably, the prisoners don't want anything that reminds them of the prison.

These rebellious activities are not confined to the UK. They are occurring all over Europe and of course in the USA where it has been said the situation in some parts is so 'bad' that teachers have to 'teach' from inside a cage-like structure. I have not been able to verify whether there really are any such situations. However a US paper, the National Enquirer, reported on 29 July 1986 : 'Violence raging out of control in our schools.'

DO TEACHERS WORK?

Some teachers argue that they are 'working class' because they work and get paid a 'salary' for it. A brief look at the meaning of the word 'work' shows that there are different kinds varying from 'easy work' to 'hard work'. (The opposite of 'work', in one definition, is probably 'idleness', though there is no 'easy idleness' or 'hard idleness', except in the sense that some enjoy idleness and some don't.)

An activity that you dislike doing, or even hate and that you would not do if you had the choice of getting paid the same for not doing it, is 'work'. But the opposite - that is an activity that you enjoy doing, that gives a sense of pleasure and/or satisfaction, and/or achievement, something that you would want to continue doing whether or not you got paid for it - surely ought not to be described by the same word 'work'.

However, the vast majority of teachers do in fact work, since most of them dislike children - some intensely - and only like teaching insofar as it gives them a feeling of power, superiority and influence that they would not otherwise have: and into the bargain they are not at all low paid and get much longer holidays than most other people. Even so all this by no means makes them 'working class'.

Teachers being somewhere near the bottom of the middle class occupational hierarchy, are often taunted by other more snooty and ignorant members of their class. For instance a jibe they often use to sneer at teachers is; "Those who can, do. Those who can't, teach". The point is that teachers both can and do indoctrinate working class children in the way described above. They can't excuse themselves; for their contribution in sustaining the dominance of their class is invaluable to their class.

Admittedly, some more-liberal teachers do find themselves in a bit of a quandary in that they are both victims of the middle class administrators' decisions, and also their agents in that they always eventually carry them out. Look at their campaign (1985) of slightly lessened co-operation, half day strikes and so on. One of the original major reasons for their action was their discontent at 'worsening conditions'. But this was eventually watered down by channelling the campaign mainly into a demand for far higher pay. And what was one of their chief arguments? It was that their demands must be met so that they could get back to 'normal working' with a higher morale and a more real feeling of being 'professionals', thus enabling them to more efficiently enforce the sort of pupil - discipline that large sections of their class are howling for.

HELP THE TEACHERS?

We should no more assist teachers in such campaigns than we should assist the police in their campaigns for similar things. Though we should bear in mind that the police are enemies of the working class who are seen as such by large numbers of people - even if, by some, only at the times when the police are more openly playing their main role of safe-guarding the interests of the middle class 'managers' of this society, like during strikes and demonstrations, or when things are being liberated from supermarkets etc... Teachers on the other hand, are generally only seen as enemies when at school. Like so many other rotten and painful experiences, once school is left behind, the distress, suffering, misery and sadness it once caused is thrust into the subconscious, is forgotten. The few good times only being remembered.

No working class activist who is truly concerned with the 'emancipation' of our class should have anything whatever to do with teachers' campaigns other than to condemn them. There is only one way of improving the education system and that is to get rid of it, lock, stock and barrel.

If you hear the squeaky little voices of middle class 'liberals' saying "But what are you going to put in its place?" tell them to just piss off and take their whimpering round to the next meeting of the amateur dramatics society because we're not going to get bogged down in that silly level of discussion. The fact is that once working class people begin on the fundamental changes necessary, they will decide. Methods of education where children are free will only be one of a myriad of things that will be changed and improved, and things will go on changing, go on improving.

sexually transmitted diseases

THE ROLE OF THE TELEVISION MEDIUM

Another middle class 'institution' that in ways is akin to the education system, and that must totally be got rid of as a priority, is the media, i.e. the mediums of the press* (newspapers, magazines, etc.), radio, television, films, videos. A medium, in this particular sense, is an agency through which those involved - as well as those in control of it - propagate their ideas, their views, their culture, (just as those in 'education' do) in order to reinforce and sustain the present kind of society.

WHOSE FREEDOM OF THE PRESS?

* As we've already seen, owners of firms and companies give orders, when it suits them, to their company chairman, who give orders to their directors, who give orders to their assistant directors, and so on. Likewise, newspaper owners give orders to their editors, who give orders to sub-editors, who.... Though rarely do newspaper owners need to give orders, for editors generally know exactly what the owners want. Indeed, one of the main qualifications for getting the job as editor is the ability to convince the owner that his newspaper will be broadly the sort of paper he wants, both in politics and financial return.

The whole of 'the press', both local and national, is owned and run solely by middle class people all of whom are totally opposed to any action which they believe might in any way contribute to the aim of working class freedom. Hence, their press is used to ensure the dominance of their class. 'The Freedom of the Press' we hear so much about, is nothing more than 'the freedom' of these people - the middle class owners and managers of 'the press' - to run it in their way for their ends.

Here, however, we shall look at only one of these media in more detail - that of television. Apart from schooling, this medium is particularly influential and effective in conditioning people to see themselves, society, and the world, in a certain way - and that way is through the eyes of the dominant class.

THE LEAD-UP TO TELEVISION

To get television and its role into some sort of perspective, it's necessary to go back a few years - to the start of radio broadcasting. The British Broadcasting Corporation, which was set up in January 1927, took over from the British Broadcasting Company. The latter was a cartel of radio manufacturers who had ganged up in 1922 with two main aims: (1) to broadcast programmes so that more people would buy their wireless sets, and (2) to get the government to impose import controls to combat what they called 'unfair competition' from manufacturers in the United States, Germany, and

Austria.

The formation of the Corporation freed the cartel members from the cost of producing and broadcasting programmes so that they were able to concentrate all their resources on the rapidly expanding market for wireless sets, while at the same time having at least one influential finger in the government-made BBC pie. For the BBC's first government-appointed Director General was none other than John Charles Reith, who until then had been General Manager of the cartel.

> **NOTE**: Reith got a knighthood in 1927 for his services to the middle class during the General Strike. Later, was chairman of Imperial Airways 1938-40; Minister of Works 1940-42 (made a 'Lord' in 1940); Director of Combined Operations Material at the Admiralty 1942-45; Chairman of the Commonwealth Telecommunications Board 1946-50, then became Chairman of the Colonial Development Corporation.

THE LIE OF 'INDEPENDENCE'

The lie that the BBC is 'independent' was propagated right from the start (just as it still is today) regardless of the fact that all its directors are virtually appointed by the government, and that Reith was made a 'Sir' by Baldwin's Conservative government for his 'good work' against the working class during the 1926 General Strike.

Winston Churchill, Home secretary at this time, was pestering the government to take over the cartel's broadcasting services as a government radio station, but Baldwin knew he could rely on Reith to do 'the right thing'. Reith himself later confirmed this when, writing about the possibility of being taken over, and about the cartel's role in the General Strike, he said: "They want to be able to say that they did not commandeer us - but they know that they can trust us not to be really impartial." (See 'The Reith Diaries', Collins 1975, p.96). So it's not surprising that he always saw the BBC as "an instrument for educating the masses." (Incidentally, another Director General again let the cat out of the bag more recently when he said that the BBC is 'a powerful and efficient instrument which has all the appearance of independence, but which the government can control at will.')

Of course, as was said earlier, it cannot be otherwise - you just can't have a neutral, independent broadcasting organization in a society dominated by the middle class. Just look at some of the rogues who were appointed to the BBC's first board of directors: The Earl of Clarendon - ex-Conservative whip in the House of Lords - became chairman; Lord Gainham - a colliery owner who, for many months in 1926, was among those ruthlessly trying to starve the miners back to work; Sir Gordon Nairne - onetime controller of the Bank of England; Dr. Montague Rendall - ex headmaster of Winchester College, one of the most expensive and the oldest public school in England; and the same sort are on the board today.

However, the government felt that they had to have on this particular board somebody reliable who was connected, if only in some vague way, with the working class, so they chose Ethel Snowden - and you couldn't get a much vaguer connection than that. She was the well-off middle class wife of Phillip Snowden, the Labour party's first Chancellor of the Exchequer in 1924, and again 1929-31. Snowden was the shit who - as Chancellor again in the National Government - introduced savage anti-working-class financial measures, and who in 1931, after cutting the unemployment benefit, was made a viscount for his 'services'.

As was said, the BBC's various boards of directors have, to this day, contained only these sorts of people, and it is they who ensure that all those in the Corporation who have any kind of influence in the producing and broadcasting of radio and television programmes, come from a certain kind of family and educational background (public school, university), have the 'right' references, and have a view of society similar to their own.

LEARNING TO DO 'THE RIGHT THING'

This 'ensuring' begins with an 'initial screening' where the appointments department excludes those who, on paper, don't appear to have the above-mentioned 'qualifications'. The interview board then questions the candidates in a similar way to Civil Service boards for senior posts. Even some of those who get through this successfully are later eliminated when the board discusses whether the candidate has a 'qualification' which the BBC considers to be one of the most important, i.e. 'will s/he make good BBC material?', in other words, does s/he show a readiness and ability to undergo the process of institutionalization - of being 'moulded' into a BBC-person who will always know 'the right thing to do' in any circumstance or situation?

However, before this 'moulding' starts, there is yet another screening that the so-far-successful candidates have to go through, this time by the State security services - who, incidentally, also investigate and report on the performers employed both by the BBC and the IBA - which is further proof that these broadcasting organizations are neither independent nor neutral. Again, it could not be otherwise, for TV and radio are important instruments in the arsenal of a dominant class who will do all they can to ensure that they remain securely in their hands.

Although there are non-official secrets such as political deals between the leaders of the political parties, and between government ministers and big commercial firms etc., about which the class-loyalty of the programme-makers has to be relied upon in coming to the 'correct' decision on how far to go, or whether to go at all, there is also the so-called classified information which can also become known to programme-makers.

Take just one area: the BBC's (and the IBA's) intricate connections with the Ministry of Defence - their involvement with, for example, secret 'emergency propaganda arrangements', and the MOD's complex communications system. My informant knows for a fact (and it's obvious anyway) that the BBC is an integral part of the nation-wide system of Regional Seats of Government each headed by a Regional Commissar; that in these 'secret' deep-underground headquarters, there are elaborate and sophisticated radio and television broadcasting facilities; that there are arrangements for main news-reporting to be controlled even more strictly by the government than it was during the General Strike of 1926, and the 'riots' and miners' strike of the 80's; that there are plans and preparations for the BBC and the commercial companies of the IBA to work in close collaboration with the government, the army, the police, and the Regional Commissars, in the case of an 'emergency'.

So those who get through this final screen are deemed to be 'secure' and are ready for 'moulding'. Although this is done formally by internal training courses, it is also done informally through the people they work with and whom they meet in the canteen, their club, even the local pub. This is the way they learn that a particular story or programme they think is 'good', is not; why a certain piece of film is unsuitable for a particular programme; whether or not, in certain situations, the Corporation will be 'liberal'; which people shall be referred to or described in a hostile way, and which in a sympathetic way; which people are 'suitable' for a particular interview - radio or television.*

* NOTE: Television service began from Alexandra Palace in North London on 2nd November 1936. Virtually all that is said here applies equally to radio. Local radio and TV are to some extent training grounds for the national networks, which no doubt accounts for the snivelling toadies we see and hear locally.

There are many more examples of what 'the good BBC person' can and cannot do, and new entrants have to learn all this very quickly if they're not to get stuck near the bottom rung of the shit-covered promotion ladder. Of course, most of them do learn quickly because, being middle class, they already know their role, and as has been said, it was ensured at the outset that they had the 'qualifications' of coming from the 'right' background, social and educational, and had views about society similar to those of the people who run the Corporation.

THEIR 'COMMON SENSE'

Thus, the 'moulded' personnel - e.g. programme-editors, sub-editors, producers, directors - come to make the 'correct choices' without really thinking about it. This 'ability' becomes so much a part of them that they are able to convince themselves that their judgements and choices are merely what they call 'common-sense', that is, sound practical judgements about politics, morals, class - indeed, about all that goes on in society. So they just don't need to be involved in what has been described as 'the conscious production of propaganda statements'. Even on those rare occasions that a radical-sounding statement does get made, a little more examination will show that it doesn't amount to anything other than the usual pro-middle-class propaganda.

These 'common-sense' interpretations of what goes on in this society in particular, and the world in general - the 'good' and the 'bad' things, the 'problems', etc. - are put into images and words, and transmitted to our screens. We are expected not only to translate it all 'correctly' - in the way they want us to - but also to agree with it because it is 'common-sense', and they are quite often dumbfounded if any of us don't.

THEIR LIES DON'T ALWAYS WORK

A person involved with BBC television once said to me of his colleagues: 'They're a bloody queer lot - they live in a different world, their own world. They don't really know what's going on in the real world outside.' This no doubt has more than a little to do with why the propaganda doesn't work when they most want it to. For example, it didn't work during the wave of strikes in the winter of 1978-79 when flagrantly anti-working-class statements were put out in the guise of 'news', particularly through the programme 'Nationwide'. Nor did it work during the miners' strike of 1984-85 when middle class presenters like the sour tight-lipped Sue Lawley and the vicious-looking Nicholas Witchell of 'The Six O'Clock News' continually spewed out lies about the mining communities. You could actually see the hatred in their faces when day after day they rabbitted on about 'the public' who disapproved of and were against the strike. Yet large sections of this 'public' excluded themselves from this 'common-sense' con-trick, saw clearly through all the 'common-sense' lies coming from their TV-sets, judged them from the logic and viewpoint of their own experiences as workers - i.e. in the flood-light of their class consciousness - and carried on the fight in the face of overwhelming odds for a very long and painful time.

The 'common-sense' of television programme-makers is the 'sense' common to the middle class view, liberal or otherwise, that this society, though it has some faults, is run in the best way possible, and that the faults can be corrected by 'democratic' means - so long as these means do not interfere with their class remaining the dominant one.

NEWS - A 'BALANCING' ACT

This is quite clearly demonstrated by those involved in the selection and preparation of the 'News'. We are never told what they don't want us to know.* Their underlying aim is to keep in people's minds the notion of the invincible power and dominance of the middle class and their 'values'. The occasional reporting of, say, the court proceedings when a respected middle class protector of these 'values' - a vicar, a policeman, an MP, or a Lord - has been caught with his hand interfering under the blanket camouflage that these 'values' represent, is an essential part of the general sleight-of-hand methods. It's part of the device, part of a psychological exercise, to give the whole dirty business of 'News' the appearance of what they call 'balance'. It's like, for example, the semblance of 'balance' they believe is provided by giving the views of opposing political parties, say Labour and Tory - that is, the views of one middle class party as opposed to those of another.

CONSPIRACY OF SILENCE

There is a conspiracy - tacit though it may be - to remain silent, not report, about what the working class in other countries are doing. For instance, if we were to base our views on what the TV and press say here - or rather, don't say - we might be forgiven for believing that there is no working class in the USA; or that, if there is, they are all having such a good time that they are peaceful and contented. Yet there are many millions of them struggling to exist on a pittance of an income, as well as millions involved in strikes, factory sabotage, and other actions against the dominant middle class every day.

And how often do we hear about the millions living in poverty in a country where the middle class are the richest in the world? Even if we use the July 1986 official government figure of 8.2 million people unemployed (despite it being, like the British one, a fiddled calculation), and add a low average of 1˙ dependents for each person, we see that there are over 20 million people, virtually all working class, living on a poverty-line income. And over there, there are also many millions on low pay, as well as millions on low old-age pensions.

However, when it comes to interviewing working class people involved with a fight with their enemy, this 'balance' is ditched and the true bias sticks out a mile. Strikers, for example, are interviewed at the pit-head, factory-gate, etc., with hand-held cameras and with a lot of distracting noise and activity going on around them - distracting to us, the viewers, as well. So these working class interviewees are in a situation of clear disadvantage, in addition to the fact that they have no experience of speaking in front of camera.

On the other hand, the middle class representatives of the employers, the government, nationalized industry, or whatever, who are available for the press and TV interviews, have had training to deal with such and/or have been chosen because they're thought to have a particular 'flare' for it. The interviewers are cringing and sympathetic compared to the way they deal with working class people, and the interview generally takes place in an office, often behind a big desk with telephones, files, papers, perhaps a vase of flowers, against a background of rows of books - i.e. within a phoney, concocted aura of importance, power, and superiority. They are told in advance what questions they are likely to be asked (some actually choose the questions, for they make it clear that they'll only answer certain ones), and in most cases have quite some time to think about what replies to give - at worst, it's the twenty minutes or so that it takes to arrange the lighting equipment and cameras.

THE HIERARCHY OF NEWS

Or take the reporting of one of the most important struggles of the 80s, the great fight of the black South African working class against the vicious oppression by the middle class whites which, amid great suffering, continues day in day out. When reported at all, it often gets relegated well down the hierarchy of item-importance - and the reports in many cases are solely those released by the fascist South African authorities.

Whether an item gets reported at all depends on a BBC/IBA process known as 'gate-keeping'. This is a term taken from farming where someone operates a gate through which the animals are being driven; by moving the gate from side to side, they are separated for dipping, for market, or for killing. So we find a report of the gassing, beating, and killing of black people by the police and army in South Africa is excluded, whereas high up the list is a lengthy account about a cake - the secret ingredients, the mixing, and so on - being made by RAF cooks, to the 'personal design' of Windsor and Ferguson whose unsavoury get-together it is intended to celebrate. (I once saw an army Staff-Sergeant cook in the officers' mess spit fluently into the meal being prepared for the gentlemen - 'for luck' he said. Who knows, perhaps a little extra lucky flavour was added to this cake.)

There are, of course, reasons for TV's obsession with the Royals. Those who run it, and those who produce the programmes, being all middle class, do their damnedest to present the Royals, not merely as a 'good' image of extreme wealth, but also as representing the stability and the 'good, Christian superiority' of their class, a superiority which they are desperate to believe entitles them to dominate the working class.

Virtually everyone who appears on our screens - actresses, actors, presenters, etc. - are middle class. Even the audiences - particularly in programmes like 'Question Time' - are mostly, if not all, middle class. And this is why the vast majority of what we see ranges from the bad to the boring. The middle class are basically so fucking boring! Anything that does seem to be 'good' is only so because it has to be judged against this high and wide background of crap.

Talking of crap, you've probably also noticed how badly programmes are arranged: what is selected for transmission, what films, etc., and at what times. Well, it has already been said by others, but it's worth mentioning again here that this is the job of a middle class secret-society known as the 'programme planners'. I've asked several people connected in various ways with television, how this P.P. society goes about this planning and selection, but nobody knows. Other than what class they belong to, it's not even known who they are. 'Programme planning' is a secret as closely guarded as the production of pathogenic micro-organisms for germ-warfare weapons at Porton Down, and the plans of the police and army to deal with insurrection by the working class.

Nothing ever appears on our screens that could be truly called pro-working class. The odd programme that seems critical of middle class ideas and actions is deliberately slipped in as 'evidence' of the 'balanced, broadminded liberal' approach of the broadcasting organizations. Even the very few 'liberal' documentary films about some of the ruthless treatment meted out to the miners during the 1984-85 strike, about the provocative and savage violence of the police (see also 'Viewers Criticisms' below), about the excellent organization and action of women's support-groups in the mining areas, were shown only after the miners had been defeated and there was consequently no longer any 'danger' of such films helping with a spread of more radical ideas and actions. At best, these documentaries invited pity, sometimes even sympathy; but they were, in any case, buried in the sickening mass of pro-middle class programmes.

LIGHT - OR HEAVY? - ENTERTAINMENT

Working class women and men, black and white, are sneered at, if not directly attacked, through 'comedy' programmes like 'It Ain't Half Hot Mum', 'Mind Your Language', 'On The Buses', 'Citizen Smith', and more recently, 'Only Fools And Horses', and 'Minder'. They were funny in parts, but it was made quite clear that the working class characters were not really very nice people, and certainly not ones that decent middle class people would want anything to do with.

On the other hand, there are the 'situation comedies' showing how working class and middle class people can cooperate, yet with the inbuilt implication that somehow the middle class character is preferable; examples are 'Never The Twain' with Windsor Davies as the working class 'rough diamond' basically getting on pretty well with the ghastly ultra-posh Donald Sinden; 'Three Up, Two Down' with the middle class actor Michael Elphick playing a somewhat crude working class dad, hitting it off with the middle class actress Angela Thorne in the part of a 'frightfully refined' middle class mummy.

SIT-COMS, SOAPS, AND SATIRE

Then there are the sit-coms intended to show that the 'good' black middle class are almost as 'good' as the 'good' white middle class, of which 'The Cosby Show' is a particularly sickening example. It's about a black middle class family where the humour is the usual gooey American slush, and where they all - including the yucky 4-year-old kid - sound and behave exactly like the nerds in all the other rubbishy American white middle class family sit-coms.

No wonder it's such a success among white American middle class viewers. No wonder it has a Harvard consultant psychologist, Dr. Alvin Poussaint, vetting all the scripts. No wonder Coretta King, widow of Martin Luther King, praises it to the heavens. But it is perhaps something to wonder about that multi-millionaire Bill Cosby, star of the piece, says that its success is because "it satisfies a nation-wide yearning for a life of comfort and stability." Can the reason for saying things like that really simply be because he is very stupid? It satisfies none of the many millions of working class people in the USA who are yearning not only to get out of the misery of poverty, but are also yearning for freedom.

Soap operas, 'Coronation Street' and 'Eastenders' for instance, are often as guilty of anti-working class, racist, and sexist 'jokes' as the sit-coms. (No doubt that's why the Queen likes Coronation Street). Whether any such 'jokes' are really funny is highly questionable. Yet they are encouraged by the Radio and TV Times describing the whole of such programmes as 'funny, enjoyable, light entertainment'; and the laughter of the studio audiences is aimed at getting viewers' collusion, at manipulating them into agreement with the underlying corrupt views on the working class, race, and women. (In the United States, the laughter is dubbed onto the sound-track after the programme has been recorded, and it's also done here in some cases.)

The so-called satirical programme, 'Spitting Image', if looked at more than superficially, will be seen to have no real criticisms of anything that matters. What about the apparent lampooning of the Royals? This simply has a strong tendency to make them more endearing to the audience. But then, what else can we expect? Everybody involved in making this programme is middle class.

BLACK VIEWS?

Programmes intended for Afro-Caribbeans and Asians, such as 'Ebony', 'Black on Black', 'Bandung File', are presented by middle class Blacks and Asians, though some middle class whites are involved in the production. However, the views expressed give the impression that they are those of the Blacks/Asians and are therefore something different. But they are in fact basically the views of the lefty middle class in general.

Take the edition of 'Bandung File' that went out from Channel 4 on 26 September 1986 where several Asian parliamentary candidates for the Labour Party were interviewed. All were middle class, university-educated, spoke with posh English accents, and said almost exactly the same things as white Labour candidates - i.e. a load of shit. And the programme's rare criticisms of the regime in

South Africa and proposals concerning what should be done about it, are at best those of the Labour Left - proposals which, even if successfully carried out, would ensure that black working class people there, despite their great suffering and heroic struggle, end up by being dominated by a middle class such as those in the leadership of the African National Congress

VIEWERS' CRITICISMS?

The criticisms of viewers in programmes with silly deceptive titles like 'Postbag', 'Talk Back', 'Right To Reply', etc., are carefully selected. So you only hear those they want you to hear, and even then manipulation comes into it. Take an example from 'Right To Reply' on Channel 4 where that phoney neutral, Gus Macdonald, pretends to ensure a balanced equality between anti- and pro-establishment opinions. In 1986, the Chief Constable of Northumbria complained on 'RTR' that, in a documentary film on the miners' strike made by Ken Loach where a policeman was seen belting hell out of a picket, sound had been added - the heavy repeated thud of the weapon crashing down on the miner's head.

Ken Loach said that although it is 'legitimate' for sound to be added to film, and is often done, it was not done in this case because it had not been necessary since the 'sound' had come over loud and clear. Throughout, Ken Loach continually and persistently asked the Chief Con what action had been taken to punish this policeman for his clearly unprovoked GBH, and each time the Chief Con refused to say. Still Loach persisted, until eventually the CC said that the 'incident' had been investigated, but no action had been taken against the officer. While the Chief Con continued to rant on about sound being added, Loach kept asking why no action had been taken. But with the crafty assistance of the 'impartial' Gus Macdonald, the Chief Constable got away without answering. (The CC was later made a 'sir').

HARKING BACK TO SECURITY

But perhaps we can take some encouragement from television's eager inclination towards nostalgia - a sentimental harking back to the past in TV dramatizations of events in the Edwardian era, and those from World Wars I and II, including the fictionalized sexual activities of the British middle class in India during the time of the Raj. We got, for example, the life of Mountbatten and how this 'blue-blooded' German Royal assisted the middle class. Another example was the repeat in May 1986 of the dramatized - and certainly partly untrue - version of the 'Edward and Mrs Simpson' hanky panky which took up the bulk of three successive evenings' viewing. (By the way, such nostalgia is not confined to television. We find it in newspaper and magazine articles and the photographs in the colour-supplements, in advertising, in fashion trends, as well as in the expensive junk in the antique shops which have popped up in their hundreds over recent years.)

This somewhat romantic return to the past is perhaps less of a deliberate and cunning plot to take our minds off the intensive attack on the working class that has been going on in recent years, but is due more to the programme makers' alarm at the situation this attack is creating - a situation the outcome of which they feel most unsure about. They see it as a hazardous gamble that could just go the wrong way for their class, which their perhaps slightly more sensitive perception shows to be far more vulnerable than it appears on the surface. So they resort to escapism; to a past that ignores the class struggle - a reaching back to times where they feel their class was in a much more secure position.

The dilemma of the 'liberal' minority of the middle class is that really there is "Nothing to look backward to with pride, and nothing to look forward to with hope." (From the poem by Robert Frost 'Death of the Hired Man'.)

AFRICA – THE GREAT 'AID' COVER-UP

The more honest of this 'liberal' minority look back with guilt, possibly with shame. Some may even have felt shame at the thoroughly disgusting display of hypocrisy by their class over the nauseating 'Aid For Africa' cover-up - a swindle which will be seen to rank high on the list of middle class corruption when we look back at the true causes why many millions of women, men, and children in Africa were and still are dying of starvation in some of the worst conditions that human beings have ever endured: cold, diseased, clothed in rags, and often without the most primitive form of shelter.

This kind of suffering has been going on all over the world for centuries - chronically in South America and Asia, but probably worst in Africa. It didn't just begin at the end of 1984 when a film shown on television broke through the silence forcing shocked attention to focus on what they called 'the tragedy in Africa'. But the class of people responsible for it was enabled to further cover up the true causes through the resulting Band Aid, Live Aid, Fashion Aid, Sport Aid, and any other trendy pleasure-giving 'charity' gimmicks.

JUMPING ON THE BAND-AID WAGON

While the whole of their news media continually referred to the causes as 'famine brought about by drought', we saw the obscene spectacle of Thatcher, Steele, Kinnock, Owen, the Royals, disc-jockeys, personalities of television, radio, theatre, press, industry, pop-music, sport, the arts, and others of similar ilk, all jumping on the Band-Aid wagon-load of hypocrisy which had been set rock and rolling by a group of publicity-seeking ego-trippers. One of these was the blatantly insincere and untalented rock singer, Bob Geldof - an opportunist who was far more sincerely peeved at not being given an OBE (Officer of the Order of the British Empire) medal in the 'New Year's Honours' of January 1986 than he ever appears to be about the starving in Africa.

However, Geldof's public snivelling about the short-sightedness of the 'Honours Scrutiny Committee' (the middle class gang responsible for deciding who gets what) eventually paid off when they made up for their defective vision six months later (June 1986) with the announcement in the 'Birthday Honours' that he had got a knighthood - worth much more to him, financially, than an OBE.

IN WITH THE SCUM

We need only to look at the company he was in when these knighthoods were doled out to see further proof of what and whom he represents. Among this scum was John Paul Getty Jnr. who became a 'Sir' for being 'generous' with a tiny portion of the wealth he'd filched from the working class (which in any case helped him with his income tax 'problems'); Ian MacGregor (then Chairman of British Coal) for his active hatred of miners on strike and suffering acutely in a struggle to save their very ordinary standard of living being reduced to the poverty of the dole; Stanley Bailey, Chief Constable of Northumbria and defender of police violence, 'for services rendered....' (need we say to whom?); Graham Edward McCamley, 'for services to the beef industry', i.e. when feed, the cause of BSE, was given to beef cattle in great quantities.

So it had at last dawned on the 'Honours Scrutiny Committee' that Geldof fitted in pretty well, that he was after all a member of their class, and his activities were really to their advantage. It was therefore quite unnecessary for Geldof to prove what a good knight he'd make by thanking them so ostentatiously only a few days later (15.6.86) by publicly stating that "the IRA are among the biggest murderers on this planet." Anyone who makes statements like that is, say those who defend him, merely an ignorant idiot. This is not true. He is, in fact, a scheming arse-licker who stood to make a lot of money out of the almost incredible amount of publicity Band Aid etc. had brought him, as well as from the title.

'Oh, I say, hold on!' whine certain inane middle class liberals, 'It must be good even if, despite the hypocrisy of it, Band Aid etc. enables only a few of the starving millions to live a bit longer.' Let's be clear, this is the most that Band Aid etc. does. In fact, in 1985 alone - gold-digger Geldof's year - more than three times the total amount received by Africans from all the charities run by middle class do-gooders (including Save The Children, Oxfam, Band Aid and its successors) was clawed back by others of the Western middle classes in debt repayments, due to other forms of 'Aid' - a subject which is looked at in more detail further on.

GROVELLING GOLD-DIGGER GELDOF

Geldof, lamenting the fact that he couldn't make any big money out of the pop-music business, said: "I wanted to make money out of it, but I only ever wanted the money to enable me to do the things I want to do." (TV Times, 25-31 October 1986) Have you ever heard of anyone wanting to make money to do things they didn't want to do?

For years before Band Aid, Geldof's band, The Boomtown Rats, had been a flop. In his so-called autobiography 'Is That It?' (published in October 1986) he wrote that they'd made an album 'In The Long Grass' - but it was no go. Tracks from it released as singles - "total stiffs." "We even went out and tried to hype the second single." They got £1,000 and "went to all the stores we knew were 'chart return' shops and bought it ourselves, hoping to buy it into the charts." (p.267). But it didn't work. "We gave away a free ticket to any one of our concerts with every copy...." Still no good. "We made four superb videos.... But still nothing." (p.268). He then writes that he was getting desperate. "It was coming to the end of 1984 and I could see no prospect for the release of the album 'In The Long Grass'.... I went home in a state of blank resignation and switched on the television." (p.269). He saw the BBC film on famine in Ethiopia. Almost immediately he also saw the opportunity of the charity-business bringing big publicity, and a way at last to make money 'to enable him to do the things he wants to do'.

Geldof in school operetta and (below) dressed for the new role

He knew he was well on that way when he arrived at Buckingham Palace on 24 July 1986. There, dolled up in top-hat and morning dress - the uniform appropriate in receiving medals for service to the middle class - he was able to bow and scrape to the queen of parasites as she officially installed him as Knight Commander of the Order of the British Empire.

The squalid hypocrisy of an 'Order of the British Empire' - the building of which was a series of atrocities substantially responsible for the immense suffering of African people right up to the present day - no more deterred Geldof's drooling acceptance of it than it does any of the other phoney do-gooders. On the contrary, his adulation of the Royals sometimes gets near to extreme. In 'Is That It?' (p.411) he says: "Of all the people I have met since this (Band Aid) began. Prince Charles is without doubt the one I have been most impressed by. I find myself more in agreement with him than anybody else."

Then the money started to roll in. One of the little things he wanted to do was get married to Paula Yates - the hip, boring, middle class pop robot. So in September 1986 out in some exotic place, he spent over £75,000 on a 'quiet little wedding.' Only a month later, the afore-mentioned book was published - with his name spread across the top of the front cover, aptly in the largest gold letters - amidst a welter of publicity. This was followed by a successful "tour to packed houses in major venues" each gig ending with the Band Aid song 'Don't They Know It's Christmas?' - a successful tour due, as he admits (p.319), entirely to publicity through Band Aid. There was then a recording contract, an album, a rubbishy single in the charts, a pop video, appearances on TV chat shows (he'd earlier been on This Is Your Life), interviews in newspapers and magazines, and he "got rows of honours, medals, awards, and even honorary degrees, from all over the world." (p.428).

In fact, the middle class, liberals to fascists, swarmed round Geldof and his Band-wagon like flies round shit - and the reasons why range from feelings of guilt to unscrupulous exploitation. For example, among the flies that got a good lick of the shit were the American multi-national companies A.T. & T. and Kodak. The purpose of their frenzied participation in these 'Aids' was made clear by Dan Hovicky, 'advertising expert' and Division Manager of A.T.& T. speaking on TV's Channel 4 (19 February 1987) of A.T. & T.'s involvement with Live Aid and Sport Aid, Hovicky said: "It was a great opportunity to show to all those who matter in the world, our technical skills, abilities, and services. It was of exceptional use to us because it enabled us to put it all over while at the same time giving a clear impression that we cared."

NOSTALGIA?

As was said, through much of television drama, the middle class try to look back only at certain events - a nostalgic return to times when they felt more secure. We, however, can look back at such times without blinkers, without the need for such sickening sentimentality - without the need to deceive ourselves. So let's look back at some of the truths and atrocities that have been covered up, and in particular at the true causes of the present-day suffering of African people. We can begin with the slave trade.

This trade was becoming profitable business for the British in the 16th century. One of the earliest British companies formed specifically for the trade was chartered in 1588 by Elizabeth I - 'Good Queen Bess' as some of our school history-books lyingly called her. Other big companies began to be formed. Thus, the slave trade came to be organized as a commercial enterprise, with investors, shares, and so on. It reached its most vicious heights in the latter part of the 18th century and the first part of the 19th.

The mine and plantation owners in South America, southern parts of the United States, and the Caribbean Islands, wanted large numbers of very cheap labourers for mining copper, tin. and silver, but particularly for growing and harvesting crops like cotton, sugar, coffee, and tobacco. Heavily-armed British, French, Spanish, Portuguese, Dutch, Swedish, and Danish gunmen regularly swept into Africa seizing thousands of virtually defenceless young men and women, then shipped them, in the most appallingly savage and inhuman conditions, to the Americas and the Caribbean.

Although hundreds of thousands died on these hell-ships, it's been estimated that at least fifteen million African people survived the agony only to suffer generations of further torment and despair many thousands of miles from their homeland. The people who controlled, directed and managed this vile business at this time were all middle class - and it was all done to satisfy the greed of Europe's middle classes.

When the imprisoned Africans, many of them in chains, arrived at the plantation or whatever, they were housed in hovels, forced to work extremely long hours, were treated worse than the farm animals,

"...the prime slave of the day... not being above 25 years of age, or defective in his lips, eyes or teeth or grown grey..."

and had absolutely no protection under the law - treatment little different from that meted out to European people by the German fascists later.

For not working at the pace the management decreed, for objecting to the terrible conditions, and for many other menial 'offences', many were starved, bound with ropes, chained, beaten with clubs, whipped, tortured - sometimes to death. In fact, many were killed, and nobody lifted a finger to help them. Slaves were far better off in ancient Rome, and in Greece several hundred years BC, for the law here gave them 'human' status - for example, the right to marry, some protection against abuse, and an opportunity of eventually being freed.

The bourgeois slave-tradesmen made fantastic profits. In fact, millions of African people became the most profitable commodity - during some years, greater than sugar - for they were an unpaid and self-producing labour-force. This profit-making involved racist atrocities that rank with those committed by the German fascists, principally against the Jewish people. It was a barbarous form of racism for which the middle classes have not been made to pay - yet.

RACISM

Racism is not just the acts of individuals, it is the result of a class system which has, built into its structure, discrimination, conquest, robbery, exploitation, and the 'right' of one class to dominate the other. It is the result of a system which justifies the 'successes' of one class by the 'failures' of the other - a system which ensures the 'successes' of one class by systematically crushing the other into what it deems to be 'failure'.

In a depraved attempt to justify their atrocities against Africans, several of the middle class managers of the trade widely publicised the profound lie that Africans were sub-human heathens with an inherent inferiority - intellectually, morally, spiritually - with no culture, hence with no feelings that mattered. They were backed up by certain middle class quacks calling themselves names like 'anthropologists' and 'geneticists', who came up with false notions based on fake information about such things as physiology, molecular biology, brain structure, personality, character and behaviour of Africans, so as to arrive at a 'scientific theory' which supported the lies of their rich middle class fascist friends.

Other corrupt justifications were made by middle class filth, one such by the so-called 'educated writer', Bryan Edwards, who in 'History of the West Indies' (1794) said: "A good mind may honestly derive some degree of consolation in considering that the wretched victims of the African slave trade are being removed to a situation more desirable than that in their native Africa."

The years of the slave trade were those of the European's savage brawl for the plunder of Africa - its bloody ruthlessness muted by most middle class writers of 'history' into simply 'the scramble for Africa.' They were the years of the barbaric brutality that went on in the building of the British Empire*, the history of which, according to the school textbooks, is almost all of heroism and glory. Even Napoleon knew about these distortions when he correctly called history "a set of lies agreed upon."

> * The British Empire is said to date from the Treaty of Utrecht (1713) under which the British dominant class got immense loot, e.g. parts of the Caribbean; Newfoundland and Nova Scotia from the French; Gibraltar and Minorca from the Spanish. But to the British, the Treaty was most important in that it gave them 'the right' to supply thousands of African slaves to the Spanish colonies.

These were in fact the years of Napoleon, and of Nelson, Wellington, the Industrial Revolution, the French Revolution, of William Pitt (founder of the Tory party), George Washington (the very wealthy bourgeois 1st President of the USA), George III (who went insane). They were the years of composers such as Haydn, Mozart, Beethoven, and painters such as Constable and Canaletto - no prizes for guessing what class of people bought tickets for their concerts, and who bought the paintings.

They were also the years of a series of wars between the dominant classes of Britain and France which were fought for the control of world trade, particularly the slave and sugar trade - a control which the British eventually secured through Wellington's victory at Waterloo (1815) to become the dominant colonial power.

SLAVERY ABOLISHED - OUT OF EXPEDIENCY!

The British middle class did not finally abolish slavery until 1833; not because of the nice 'democratic' actions of a handful of middle class do-gooders (the legendary activities of MP William Wilberforce amounted to little more than sometimes speaking against it in parliament), but because their sugar plantations were at maximum production and were really able to continue without the import of more African slaves - consequently, the British were then intent upon stopping the flow of slaves to their commercial enemies, the French.

In the USA, slavery was not abolished until after the end of the Civil War in 1865, and even then, like the British, their reason was due far more to expedience than to any feelings of guilt or concern for justice. In other places, slaves were not released until much later. For example, the Portuguese in Angola decreed in 1858 that African slaves would not be set free until 1878; in parts of South America (e.g. Brazil) release did not come until near the end of the century.

NOTE: Though the racism discussed here is that committed against Africans by the European middle classes in the 18th-19th centuries, they were no more the originators of such fascist theories and actions than were the middle class German fascists lead by refuse like Goebbels, Himmler and Streicher in the 1930's. For example, there was the not-unsimilar vicious racism by the English against the Irish in the 15th and 16th centuries; and later, that of the European colonists against the American Indians - who, incidentally, had been in North America for at least 20,000 years, and probably for as long as 35,000 years.

Greek writers who, hundreds of years BC, firmly declared that the black people of Africa were the first human beings, have today been proved right. Africans are now known to have had various technologies and skills many centuries before any such appeared in Europe. There were highly developed societies in Africa thousands of years BC, and there have been many since. They learned how to use the often harsh environment to master the problems of survival and development in order to satisfy their daily needs for food, shelter, medicine, clothing, as well as for leisure and pleasure.

RACISM - A DISEASE

So it's clear that the particular form of racism described here - that directed against black people of African origin - is a middle-class-induced disease; a disease with which they, being the dominant class, have infected the class they dominate. And it still persists today - though the racist 'scientists', 'sociologists' and 'psychologists' of today put forward their so-called theories about the inferiority of black people with a great deal more difficulty in the face of ever-mounting and overwhelming evidence to the contrary.

There are even some middle class 'liberals' who, although having accepted that the idea of black people's genetic racial inferiority is a lie, have now come up with another more devious, though nonetheless fraudulent, 'theory': that they are not born inferior, but their 'cultural values' have made them inferior.

There are, of course, a few 'liberals' who genuinely try to counter racism. But this few are up against more influential members of their class. Examples are those who run 'The Sun' newspaper whose theory is that it can help to dampen down trouble from an oppressed class of people if they can be persuaded to feel racially superior to other people - Africans, Asians, South Americans, etc. They know that people want to be respected, but the middle class define respect in terms of despising someone else.

Anyway, to the middle class, that 'someone else' is not only someone of a different race, for they believe themselves to be superior to a majority of their own race. Though their belief that working class people are inferior to them is promoted more subtly, it is nevertheless quite clearly implied in written and spoken statements - how they do it through the medium of television has already been mentioned.

But the same view can easily be detected in the stuff we get from the more libertarian middle class lefties. They will give the impression that they go along with the statement that 'the emancipation of the working class is the task of the working class themselves', but they really believe that we can't free ourselves from the domination and oppression of their class without help from them. Ignoring them is one way of dealing with them - exposing them is better.

BACK TO AFRICA

But to return to the question of Africa. The slave trade vandalized a substantial part of the country. It was responsible, as we have seen, for the forcible removal of more than fifteen million men and women by the Europeans alone. Vast areas were de-populated and many communities wrecked (examples are far too numerous to be given here), thus creating local wars where before there had been peaceful development; havoc in food production was created where there had generally been sufficiency, thus inflicting famines. In fact, conditions were created from which Africans have never yet been able to recover - in many cases, have not been allowed to.

THE MISSIONARIES - DO-GOODING WITH A GUN

In the wake of the slave trade came the missionaries. Hundreds of them poured into the continent - literally with bible in one hand and gun in the other. They were going to save these pagans' souls even if they had to kill them to do so. They were going to change, by force if necessary, African belief in non-existent gods - Catholic, Protestant, Baptist, etc. And a great number of Africans were battered and killed in the name of Jesus Christ by these white, middle class, missionary barbarians.*

* HUMANITARIAN BARBARISM

In the Belgian Congo (now Zaire), white middle class Roman Catholic missionaries were encouraged by the administration on the grounds that this brand of Christianity produced Africans of a more docile and obedient type than other brands did. The Belgians had occupied this land 80 times the size of their own country, and containing a population of many millions of Africans, so control was difficult. It was under the staunch Roman Catholic Leopold II (King from 1865 to 1909) that the most hideous atrocities were committed to bring about obedience. Thousands died as a result of floggings, torture, and mutilation - hands were chopped off by the thousands - as well as from summary executions. Sir Henry Morton Stanley, though better known for finding David Livingstone, was in fact a rather more posh kind of mercenary, for he worked diligently and very effectively for Leopold II during this time.

These foul hypocrites claimed all the while that what they did was in the name of philanthropy and humanitarianism. It's not difficult to understand why Africans hated even more those Europeans who claimed 'humanitarianism' as the spur to actions which were aimed at subduing them and plundering their country.

All this directly contributed to the further horrors suffered by Africans in Zaire following 'independence' in 1960 when, for example, Moise Tshombe hired white fascist mercenaries to put down rebellions as ruthlessly as possible - an example of yet another decadent legacy of white middle class ideas and administration, for here too the scum still rose to the top.

Their role though was something much more than just beating the gospel into the pagans. To become 'genuine god-fearing Christians', the 'black heathens' had to become white-fearing believers in carefully-selected parts of what Jesus Christ is said to have taught, like the importance of being meek and docile, turning the other cheek and so on, but certainly not bits like all people being equal. To become genuine Christians, they had to become Europeanized. They therefore had to be indoctrinated with European middle class ideas, one of the most important which was that the missionaries, themselves all middle class, were better than the Africans, were far superior, and that they therefore had a God-given right to dominate those they decided were their inferiors.

NOTE: This attitude of racial and class superiority prevails to this day among virtually all the whites in South Africa, almost all of whom are Christians.

The fact that the African National Congress, formed in 1912, for fifty years duped black South African working class people into believing that they could get freedom by peaceful means, is in no small way due to several of the ANC's leaders having been 'educated' by missionaries; also that these missionaries recorded their greatest number of 'converts' in South Africa. No doubt these 'converts' thought it was better to get baptised with a gun in your back than to have a bullet through your heart.

The way black Africans conducted their lives, their traditional beliefs, customs, knowledge, and skills - what the sociologists would call 'their culture' - were not to the advantage of the European classes in their drive to exploit Africa and its people. So the people were labelled as bad, pagan, heathen, evil, anti-Christ, etc., and therefore had to be 'educated'.

The form and purpose of this 'education' of Africans in the latter half of the 19th century was little different from those in this country then and today. Rule by the white middle class had to be sustained by creating among the ruled a kow-towing respect for the rulers. 'Education' had to be such that the pupil 'learnt' that s/he was inferior, and either could never attain the 'superior culture' of the European middle classes, or only stood a chance of doing so provided traditional beliefs and 'culture' were abandoned, thus becoming, as has been said, Europeanized - which, in effect, meant economically and socially under the heel of these European whites.

An element in the missionaries education drive was the creation of a black middle class, though some European governments (e.g. Britain and France) were indecisive in their support of this. It was an indecision influenced by the colonialist settlers who, since they saw black Africans purely as a cheap labour-force, were strongly opposed to such 'ignorant meddling' as they called it.

Let's be quite clear, the missionaries did no good whatever, even unintentionally. Anything which, viewed in isolation, might appear to be 'good' - like for example the introduction of certain medicines - was totally offset and invalidated by the rottenness of the system they so effectively helped to introduce. It's not 'good' to give people aspirins while contributing to their enslavement and suffering.

Of course, the white colonialists did not oppose the missionaries' medicines. They knew - like those who introduced the Welfare State here - that people can't be exploited efficiently if they are sick.

THE PLUNDERING COLONIALISTS

So, the missionaries paved the way for the European middle classes' colonialization - yet another form of enslavement. Just as 'Good Queen Bess' gave charters to slave-trading companies in 1588, so were colonialist companies given charters in the 1800's.

It was towards the end of that century that one of the worst of British colonialist filth, Cecil Rhodes, got a Royal Charter for his British South Africa Company from the Conservative prime minister, Lord Salisbury (see also 'Bloodthirsty Tory Leech' p.88). Rhodes - whose 'success' was significantly due to the collusion of the missionaries - was a ruthless middle class tyrant motivated entirely by a gluttonous

Cecil Rhodes'
dirty dream

and limitless greed for wealth and power, in pursuit of which no kind of action was too cruel, vicious, depraved, or barbaric. In comparison to Rhodes, Attila the Hun and Genghis Khan caused less suffering and had better ideals.

The colonialization of Africa by the European middle classes was achieved solely by an overwhelming supremacy in weapons for killing Africans who in any way resisted. As one English middle class poetical hack wrote at the time:

"Whatever happens we have got
The Maxim gun and they have not."

THE MAXIM GUN
Invented in 1883 by an American, Hiram Maxim, who had earlier settled in London. Mass-produced by Vickers, it was the first machine-gun to use successfully the recoil energy of the fired bullet to eject the shell and put another cartridge into the firing chamber. Maxim got a knighthood for it.

SHRAPNEL
Another 'great invention' used at the time was the exploding shell. Its middle class inventor was Henry Shrapnel (1761-1842) who got the 'bright idea' of putting a number of bits of sharp metal into a casing together with a charge of powder fired by a time fuse. When the shell burst, its contents showered into the people around.

Thus, by the turn of the century (1900) the whole of Africa (except Ethiopia and Liberia) had been subjugated and brought under the control of the middle classes of seven European countries - Britain, France, Spain, Portugal, Germany, Italy, and Belgium. This was the essence of colonialism - the forcible extraction of wealth from conquered peoples. And here originated the main causes of the millions dying from starvation: cash crops.

But before looking at how 'cash crops' cause famines, something must be said about the situation in South Africa.

MIDDLE CLASS BARBARISM IN SOUTH AFRICA

In South Africa, the white Dutch/British middle class have violently driven 20 million black Africans (nearly 75% of the population) into areas comprising only about 7% of the land - land which is of poor quality, much of it infertile, and which consequently has had to be massively over-cultivated, and which also has no mineral wealth. The whites have stolen the remainder - land where the soil is exceptionally rich for agricultural production, and where the mineral wealth (gold, diamonds, coal, iron) is phenomenal.

Not content with the suffering this robbery caused, the whites inflicted further misery by taxing village huts, with the penalty of beatings and imprisonment for not paying enforced by the white police and army. This, together with the impossibility of living off the land, forced about half the South African population to travel, often long distances, to work in the factories, mines, farms, and households of this white middle class trash. These millions of workers are compelled to live in 'white' urban areas for long periods, in atrocious conditions, with virtually no rights, and a pittance in wages.

Gold-mining is a flagrant example of their total unconcern for the welfare and safety of black workers. It was for precisely these reasons that the fire at the Kinross gold-mine in September 1986 killed 172 black miners. Next to this mine, 7,000 miners are crammed into harshly-austere barrack-like buildings and are forbidden by law to have their wives and/or families with them. Over the years, in the gold-mines alone, many thousands have been killed - nearly a thousand a year - and many more thousand are injured.

The situation of black South Africans is relatively as bad as, if not worse than, that of the slaves 150 years ago - and they are kept in this hell by a ruthless, Fascist, middle class regime.

THE BRITISH INVOLVEMENT

It must not be forgotten that the British middle class laid the foundation for all this. Alfred Milner, British High Commissar, then later Governor of South Africa, referring to their plans for that country, said in 1908: "The ultimate end is a self-governing white community supported by well-treated black labour."

Evidence of how well this treatment was to be, was seen in one of the first measures taken by the new Union Parliament: the Land Act (finally passed in 1913) limited the land the Africans could buy for their own occupation to little more than 7% of the entire land area of the country - and the poorest land at that. Thus, the white middle class, legalized' their theft of some 90% of the best land.

NAMIBIA TOO!

The South African middle class also control Namibia to the north west of the country. Here, 1˚ million Africans are subjugated in a similar hell by over 100,000 heavily-armed South African troops. Namibia, as well as South Africa, produces more wealth for the white middle classes than any other African country; minerals such as diamonds, lead, and uranium are abundant, and the vast areas of cattle and sheep farming land are of the highest quality. The great majority of Namibians, however, live in a poverty so agonizingly severe that it ranks with the worst in the world.

The country - originally colonised by the German middle class and called German South West Africa - has been occupied by South African regimes since 1915. Following the end of World War I (1920), the representatives of the world's various middle classes who made up the so-called League of Nations, formally took South West Africa from Germany and gave the British a mandate to govern it. The British handed the country over to the South African whites to govern on their behalf. In 1966, the United Nations Organization ended the mandate and ordered the South African government to completely withdraw, but they completely ignored the order. In 1971, the all-middle-class International Court of Justice at the Hague declared the South African occupation illegal. Again, their class-counterparts in South Africa stuck two fingers up.

The British middle class support this vicious plundering of Namibia in that they are deeply involved in it. Some fifty British companies are still robbing the Namibians of their country's wealth - and the taxes etc. which these companies pour into the coffers of Botha's Fascist regime pay for its vast army of occupation in Namibia. This is no surprise. There is no limit to what any of the world's middle classes will do - despite the few 'liberals' amongst them who in any case never do anything to effectively impose a limit - to sustain and increase their economic and social dominance.

THE AFRICAN NATIONAL CON

The African National Congress (ANC), formed in 1912* to change all this, is controlled by a black middle class - teachers, lawyers, clergymen, chiefs - many of whom were and still are missionary-educated Christians. For the following fifty years, their policies of non-violence and passive-resistance did not simply change nothing, but the living conditions of the great black majority got steadily worse.

Albert Luthuli, president of the ANC from 1952 to 1960, was a staunch missionary-educated Christian dedicated to non-violence, a school-teacher before becoming a Zulu chief, and winner of the white middle class's Nobel Prize 'for outstanding work in promoting peace' - in his case, for his worse than ineffective pacifism, for he was doing a good job for the whites.

* Later, in Namibia, the South West Africa People's Organization (SWAPO) was formed.
PRIZES FOR SERVICES TO....?
Alfred Bernard Nobel (1833-96) of Sweden founded the Nobel Prizes through his will. Nobel invented dynamite, and a more powerful form of gelignite. He also produced ballistite, one of the first nitro-glycerine smokeless powders. Through the manufacture of these he became a millionaire.

When Luthuli was banned in 1960, Nelson Mandela took over. Mandela had been to the university at Fort Hare, and then became a lawyer with a business practice in which Oliver Tambo (current ANC president) was his partner.

When South Africa left the Commonwealth in May 1961 and became a republic, Mandela called a general strike, but it was a failure. This didn't mean that, due to the influence of the ANC, black South Africans had become 'pacified', cowed, and were afraid; on the contrary, angry demonstrations had been taking place in various parts of the country for some time - earlier at Sharpville, for example, a demonstration by a big crowd of unarmed people had been attacked by police who

Sharpville,
March 1960

fired on them. Killing 70 (among them 8 women and 10 children), and wounding nearly 200.

So Mandela and others of the ANC leadership, to keep their positions, were pushed into renouncing non-violence. Eventually (1964), Mandela - since the regime believed he had become a symbol of stiffer black resistance - was arrested, 'tried', and sent to Robben Island for life. (It's reported however that he is today in Pollsmoor Prison, Capetown.)

THE ONLY WAY!

The only way the black working class can get freedom in South Africa is by the complete overthrow of the whole white middle class. In this 'task', not only must no reliance be put on any help from the black middle class - whose main concern, no matter how liberal or revolutionary some of them may appear to be, is to get themselves into positions of power afterwards - but they too must be overthrown.

> **NOTE**: The white middle class may have caused possibly insurmountable problems for themselves by not creating a large and powerful enough black middle class - as, for example, the British had achieved in India by the time of 'Independence' in 1947.

Together with a growing political awareness, the forcible herding of millions of Africans into the so-called 'white urban areas' has had effects which may well prove to be important factors in bringing about this only way to freedom. One effect has been to weaken the influence of the black middle class 'leadership', as well as that of black teachers, education officials, councillors, police, and businessmen. A number of instances of this have been seen over the last couple of years. One such was at a big rally in 1986 when another Nobel Prize winner (1984) and well-known 'leader', Bishop Desmond Tutu, was speaking. Several sections of the crowd openly ignored him by turning their backs, singing and dancing.

> **TUTU WORRIED BY THE 'MOB'**
>
> In reference to the arrests of black 'leaders' that had been taking place, Bishop Tutu said on BBC radio 16 June 1986: "I am worried because they have taken away the leadership of a community, and it could turn into a mob."
>
> At around the same time, another 'leader' - Murphy Morobe, publicity secretary of the United Democratic Front which collaborates with the 'liberal' white middle class - said: "The removal of the leaders increases the risks of the mobs running wild."
>
> The 'mob' they and the white fascist leaders refer to with such fear is, of course, the working class.

There have also been an ever-increasing number of attacks on police-informers and collaborators, as well as black police and councillors, some having the homes and businesses smashed and burnt, dozens being killed.

Another effect has been that, due to having to live in the 'white areas' for long periods, families have been split up, thus undermining the bourgeois teaching (both Christian and fascist) about the importance of strict parental control. This has enabled young people more clearly to see such dogmatic teaching for what it is - a means for sustaining the dominance of the white (and black!) middle class.

LIBERATION BEFORE EDUCATION

One of the results of this was seen at Soweto in 1976 where, despite the hitherto moderating influence of the South African Students' Union, the revolt of thousands of school-children (almost as many girls as boys) against the white-imposed education system turned into violent opposition to everything else - to the whole economic and political system. The police of the white middle class fascists killed 600 children and wounded many more.

Soweto,
June 1976

The revolt spread and exploded in townships, as well as the so-called homelands, throughout South Africa, with hundreds of schools, administration buildings, courts, and shops, being burnt to the ground. This, and the 'school-boycott' under the slogan 'Liberation Before Education', has continued sporadically ever since[1]. In fact, due to the radical anti-middle class attitude and consequent actions of young black people such as 'The Comrades' centred around the massive Crossroads Squatter Camp complex on the outskirts of Capetown, it reached a point where townships were taken over, and they became no-go areas not only for the whites' security forces, but also for the black collaborators.

[1] Of the 25,000 black South Africans imprisoned without trial since the so-called emergency was declared in 1986, over 12,000 are children.

Of course, the black middle class - though treated as inferior by the whites - have a vested interest in anything that opposes the only way, and in recent years some have formed themselves into organizations of which perhaps 'The Fathers' is the best known here. Some are nothing more than groups of thugs hired by well-off blacks to enforce 'protection rackets', and to extort money from black working class people in other ways, such as rent for squatting, as in the Crossroads Camp. One 'Fathers' leader, for example, is Johnson Ngxobongwana, a so-called 'property baron', who can often be seen driving around the Camp in a large gold Mercedes, obviously in collusion with the security forces.

'The Comrades', who represent the mood of the vast majority of young black people throughout the country, were seen by the whites for what they had become: a serious threat, not just to the dominance of their class, but to their very survival. 'The Comrades' therefore had to be suppressed.

Early in 1986, 'The Fathers' - who had been at loggerheads with 'The Comrades' for some time - did a deal with certain sections of the whites' security forces and, many of them armed with guns, went on the rampage through the main camp and the four satellite camps. With the help of Botha's forces - often quite openly with rifles, tear-gas, and flame-throwers[2] - 'The Fathers' gradually got the upper hand. Seventy-two people were killed, hundreds were wounded; half the makeshift hovels were destroyed, thus making over 70,000 people homeless, or rather, hovelless. All those ousted have been warned, both by 'The Fathers' and the white authorities, that they risk their lives if they return.

[2] The overwhelming proof of this on film and video, as well as from everyone interviewed in the Crossroads camps, forced those of TV and press who select and prepare news reports in this country to stop referring to the battles as 'tribal fighting'.

But the millions of young working class people of South Africa, together with many of the older ones, have neither been defeated or demoralized. And their enemies - not just those in South Africa, but the middle class regimes, black and white, in the rest of the world - know this only too well. They know that a massive violent uprising is now more likely than ever before unless....... unless these working class people can somehow be manipulated into believing the lie that some concessions on Apartheid actually amount to sure steps in the direction of real emancipation.

APARTHEID

Apartheid is a term first used in 1929 to mean the separation of the dominated black Africans (90% of the population) from the dominating white ex-Europeans - in other words, blatant racism. When Daniel Malan, leader of the Nationalist Party, became prime minister in 1948, this 'separation' was enforced with a far greater aggressive and ruthless violence, and has been ever since.

It means that black South Africans have virtually no rights, and have to live in squalor and poverty while the whites have one of the highest standards of living in the world.

Various notorious European and US representatives of the middle classes - such as the British Foreign Secretary, Geoffrey Howe, and the US secretary of State, George Schultz - say they want 'concessions' on Apartheid, by which they mean, at most, some bait, some trick, some kind of deception, some sort of blindfolding exercise such as the introduction of a way which will allow a few of the black middle class into the white South African government. We can only hope that their swindling strategy fails.

THE 'SANCTIONS' DRUG

So to try to get the Botha regime to relax the Apartheid laws a bit, several of the middle class governments around the world, including some in other African countries, waffle on about applying certain economic penalties against the regime - possible cuts in things they buy off them, or export to them. 'Sanctions' they call it, and they try to make it sound as if they're serious.

'Sanctions' is one of the drugs in a manipulatory formula. Many, if not all, of these 'sanctions' pushers are aware that the fascist Botha regime - depending as it does on ultra-fascists like those of Eugene Terre Blanche's Africaner Resistance Movement - is emotionally intellectually, hence politically, unstable. They also think that the regime's backs-to-the-wall resistance to any reform which might lead to even only a few middle class blacks in the government, may well contribute to an insurrectionary upheaval the outcome of which could mean not only the loss of the great commercial value that South Africa is to them, but also quite possibly to the loss of their class's dominant position in their own societies.

The Kaundas and Mugabes of Africa seem to know this. The seven members of the so-called Eminent Persons Group most certainly do. They got together in 1986 to go out there in an almost desperate attempt to find a solution to a situation the possible consequences of which most of the world's middle classes fear would seriously affect them.

Just look at who these 'eminent' middle class persons were - and then at what they proposed for a 'solution'.

The group included Archbishop Scott of Canada - to give it the eminent parson touch; Malcolm Fraser - rich, Oxford educated, member of a wealthy sheep-farming family, and former prime minister of Australia; and Lord Barber - as plain Mr. Anthony Barber in the early 70's, was a Tory Chancellor of the Exchequer, and is now chairman of the Standard and Chartered Bank which, together with Barclays, controls 60% of banking in South Africa.[3] The Group's proposals included the legalization of the African National Congress (which is really the equivalent of the Labour Party in South Africa), and the release of Nelson Mandela. In exchange, the ANC would revert to a policy of non-violence and begin peaceful negotiations with the Botha fascists. There can be no doubt that the ANC had agreed to this, for the Eminent Persons had had several meetings with ANC leaders, including Mandela whom they met in prison in March and May of that year (1986). After these meetings, they stated that Mandela had said he was "ready to seek a negotiated solution." Indeed, Bishop Tutu is now (March 1987) calling for the ANC to go back to its policy of non-violence.

[3.] **THE BRITISH INTEREST**

Of the 2,000 companies in South Africa which are owned by middle class people of other countries, over 50% are British. Direct investment of those of other countries in things like factories, plant, and equipment, is in the region of £12,000 million, of which some 40% (£5,000 million) is British.

On 24 November 1986, Barclays Bank announced that they were beginning a gradual pull-out of South Africa 'for strictly commercial reasons'. It's true that one of the 'commercial reasons' is that their profits have been declining. But whether it's true or not that they are in fact pulling out, it's useful for them to say so. They know there is going to be a 'change'. If it is the one they all hope for - namely, the bringing of some middle class blacks into government to stabilize the situation - then, Barclays think they will be regarded in a better light by blacks (due to the stated 'pull-out'), and the way back into the big profits will be made that much easier.)

WHO WILL THEY BACK?

Of course, it's still possible that Botha and his middle class vandals may see the light (a vision of the 'white' areas of Johannesburg, Pretoria, and Capetown in flames maybe) and join in the negotiating game - for they may well still be able to remember how usefully the ANC served them during the first 50 years of its existence.

Will the apparent flies in the ointment, Reagan and Thatcher, eventually be dug out? Who knows? The thick slimy streak of fascism running through them is, after all, only a reflection of the same streak that runs through most middle class elites. (To look at only one reflection: what about his hollow holiness the Pope giving the fascist Pinochet 'the papal blessing' in Chile on 3 April 1987?). They are all, therefore, to varying degrees, also unstable. They believe, if not they can always win, that at least they can never lose. So some of them may well stick with the Botha hoodlums.

They are, however, all dogged by the same dilemma that whereas the policies and actions of the South African fascists could more than likely lead to the very insurrection they all fear, it is nevertheless by no means certain that the 'leaders' of the African National Congress and the United Democratic Front could restrain those they call 'the mob', the working class. But some choice has to be made, so many of them will no doubt go for those they think most likely to succeed - the ANC and the UDF.

MANY WORKING CLASS PEOPLE STILL BLINKERED

No-one can really blame the working class of South Africa if they are conned into believing that these middle class organizations will lead them to freedom. They've been similarly conned in other parts of Africa - just as the working classes have all over the world. In this country, large numbers of our class still have illusions, still remain deceived, about several things - the true nature of middle class 'democracy', to name but one.

Nigeria's Major-General Ibriham Babangida (right), the country's sixth military leader since independence in 1960, assumed power in August last year by staging a coup d'etat. In 25 years the continent has seen 70 coups, and a third of African countries are now under military rule

We and our black sisters and brothers in Africa have a common enemy, but the obstacles facing them are greater; they must defeat the black as well as the white middle class. For although many have been forced to see the white middle class for what they are, they still do not look at things in class terms generally. Many of them still do not see the black middle class as their enemies, despite the often glaring example of this in other parts of Africa. They still do not seem to see them as enemies who will use - whenever they think it necessary for the survival of themselves and their dominant position - every conceivable means to keep it that way, i.e. every possible means to keep the working class suppressed.

There is also 'the lesser of two evils' argument to be overcome - in their case, the delusion, the fallacy, that it is better to be dominated and bossed around by blacks rather than whites.

THE LESSER OF TWO EVILS

This 'argument' - first put forward by Aristotle 300 years BC when he said "Of evils we must choose the least" - is one still put forward in this country today, often by otherwise reasonable political activists, as grounds for voting for the Labour Party. It's an argument which not only causes confusion, but worst, one that strengthens and magnifies an illusion.

And this delusion itself is underpinned by those elitist political manipulators out there who say that the 'lesser of two evils' fallacy can only be exposed by taking the black working class through the experience of black middle class government - an argument similar to that of their counterparts here such as the Trotskyists in parties like the Socialist Workers' Party.

The middle class leaders of such parties propagate the 'theory' that the working class must become involved in bourgeois democracy and strive to get a Labour Party government so as to 'take them through the experience' which will enable them to see more clearly that the crap middle class Labour Party cannot bring them freedom, whereas their crap middle class 'revolutionary' parties can.

WORSE ENEMIES!

These people and their organizations are as much the enemies of the working class as are the Tories, the Labourites, the SDP-ers, or the Liberals. In fact, they are worse, in the sense that they claim to be working class parties (note: today the Labour Party itself no longer claims to be that), yet they are controlled mainly by middle class people who say - and some actually seem to believe - that they know what is best for the working class. This is a form of arrogant elitism which produces bourgeois analyses and theories - like, for example, 'democratic centralism'* - thus contributing to the general confusion of working class people, but in particular to that of could-be real revolutionary activists.

* 'Democratic Centralism' is the management method of, for example, the Socialist Workers' Party, where the decisions are taken by the middle class leadership, and only after they have been implemented can they be checked for 'correctness' by the rank and file - clearly demonstrating their calculated deception that 'the emancipation of the working class' is only possible with them as leaders.

FAMINE IN AFRICA

THE 'CASH-CROPS' CAUSE

To return to how 'cash crops' cause famine. Cash crops are the things that people have been, and still are, forced to grow so as to get money to pay off loans, and to pay rents to the landlords. It was even happening in Ireland 140 years ago. During the famine there from 1846 to 1850, food enough to feed double the population of 8 million was exported while two million people died of starvation. The famines of 1876 to 1879 in India caused the deaths of over 6 million people, while at the same time the British shipped some 4 million tons of grain to their home country via the recently opened Suez Canal (1869). These millions of people, like the millions in Africa, died slow agonizing deaths. Was the killing of 6 million people by the German fascists really worse?

In a letter to the Colonial Office of the French government, dated 7 March 1932, even a middle class 'Inspecteur' in the famine-stricken French 'possession' of Upper Volta (now Burkina Faso) in N.W. Africa felt compelled to write:

"One can only wonder how it happens that populations whose policy had always been to have three harvests in reserve, and to whom it was unacceptable to eat grain that had spent less than three years in the granary, have suddenly become 'imprevoyant' (lacking in foresight). They got through the terrible drought years of 1912-1914 without hardship, now these people are starving."

"I feel morally bound to point out that the policy giving priority to industrial cash-crops has coincided with an increase in the frequency of food scarcity."

This discreet letter, ignored of course by the French government, makes it quite clear that the causes of famine and starvation were not blight, locusts, or drought - these the people knew about, had planned for, and could deal with. The causes were the greed and violence of the French middle class. The "policy of giving priority to industrial cash-crops", as the Inspecteur so politely called it, as well as that giving priority to raw materials and minerals, was going on all over Africa (as well as India and South America), consequently African people were not able to grow enough food for themselves.

A fact well known to the middle class 'agricultural experts' - so-called agronomists and such-like - is that the many large areas of good flat land in Africa will produce 3 to 5 times as much as the best land in the USA. There are also many areas of great mineral wealth. All this was seen as good profitable investment by Western middle class 'businessmen'. In a great number of cases, to enable millions of acres to be 'taken over' by their finance companies, Africans' villages were burnt down, and the villages forced at gun-point to work on plantations growing crops like coffee, cotton, rubber, as well as in the mines for minerals such as copper, cobalt, tin, gold, and diamonds. African peasant-farmers who somehow managed to escape that, were forced onto the smallest areas of poor quality land, often on steep hillsides. These are the people whom the 'agricultural experts' accuse of 'over-cultivating' and/or 'over-grazing'

- though this they are compelled to do since it is the only way they can survive.

As the above letter only vaguely hints at, the French middle class used a slightly different kind of force - taxation. With the support of their army, they compelled Africans to pay taxes to work on their own land by threatening them with imprisonment or being put into forced-labour-gangs if they didn't pay up. As the French well knew, these Africans didn't have any money, hadn't ever needed it. The 'clever' French middle class colonialists had the answer to this 'deficiency'. The Africans were told to 'stop growing things like millet and sorghum for your own consumption, and grow cotton and peanuts. These we'll then buy from you, and with the money you'll be able to pay your taxes and buy food from us.' The French did buy these 'cash-crops', but at rock-bottom prices for export to their home industries at tip-top profits.

MASTERS OF THE RIP-OFF

So with the money they got from the French, some Africans were able to give it back through paying the taxes and buying their expensive food. Cunning, eh? The middle class, while they've got the power, are masters of the great rip-off. In this case, money was introduced into societies which before hadn't needed it - the French printed it, the Africans forced to 'earn' it, and the French got it back through taxes and sales of food. A very vicious vicious-circle.

But many Africans still couldn't pay the taxes. So to survive, they had to go in search of work for wages. In addition to this, all men had to work a number of days in the year (varying from 90 to as much as 180) for the French instead of on their own little farms, on 'corvee' as it was called - a military term meaning 'fatigue duty', i.e. forced labour. As a result, the Africans' own food stores soon got used up and famine set in.

The British middle class had a similar technique in some parts of their 'possessions' for exploiting the 'natives', though often through a more hierarchical system. In India, for example, they used better-off 'natives' as the initial tax collectors - Zamindari, as they were called. These people, who had to hand in a fixed amount each year, appointed subordinates to do the collecting, who in turn also appointed subordinates, and so on down a whole chain of 'middlemen'. It is a fact that, in some areas, there were as many as 35 middlemen between the poor farmer at the bottom, laboriously scratching a miserable living out of his little plot of land, and the wealthy British viceroy at the top, sitting in luxury on his throne lazily scratching his balls. It was a cut-throat system in which each middleman could keep any money over the amount he had to pay to the one above him. This created a drive to extort the maximum, and this often led to violent conflict. It was of course a system well in line with the dominant class's theory of 'divide and rule'

Today in Africa, less than a quarter of the land good for cultivation is being used. Even if the population continues to grow at the present rate until the year 2000, there would still be the potential to feed one-and-a-half times (i.e. 50% more than) that population - and that's assuming there were only very small-scale improvements in food-production techniques.

Sure, poor people in poor countries have more children than is average in, say, Europe - they need to. Children are essential additional labour and, from quite a young age, contribute to the family livelihood. Later they provide some sort of support for their parents in old age, for there's no 'old-age pension'. And they have to have more children than they actually need for this because, due to hunger and the diseases it causes, many children die before they are five years old.

It's a fact that population growth goes down where people get some decent arable land, enough to eat, and hence better security. So the campaigners for birth control show their true colour, their hypocrisy, in that they never campaign against those members of their class who've stolen the land and demand it back as a method of birth control.

Population-growth with no increase in food production obviously makes hunger a bit worse - but it does not cause it.

BLOODTHIRSTY TORY LEECH
Lord Salisbury, who was Secretary for India before becoming Tory prime minister, said in 1875: "Since India must be bled, this should be done judiciously, and the lancet directed to those parts where the blood is congested or at least sufficient."

THE 'OVER-POPULATION' NONSENSE

Before going on to explain other aspects of the cash-crops-cause of famine, let's just explode the middle class argument that over-population is a cause. Lots of silly bastards come up with this one -

and their solution? Birth control. (Some of the more fascist among them have even advocated sterilization.) They have run campaigns for this, and even that not-so-bad middle class organization, the Red Cross, has been involved. Of course, middle class businessmen of the West have muscled in on this one too - millions of inferior 'unsafe', and some outright dangerous, contraceptives have been dumped in underdeveloped countries, at a fat profit for the businessmen.

So let's get this 'over-population' nonsense into perspective with some facts:

AFRICA COUNTRY	NUMBER OF PEOPLE PER SQUARE MILE
Uganda	140
Morocco	107
Zimbabwe	46
Tanzania	45
Zaire	30
Angola	14
Congo	11
Namibia	3

OTHERS COUNTRY	NUMBER OF PEOPLE PER SQUARE MILE
Hong Kong	11,515
Holland	880
UK	583
India	516
France	255
China	243
Brasil	38
Bolivia	12*

* NOTE: In Bolivia - centre of South America - the great majority of people are very poor, and the minority are very rich. Most of the poor are on the verge of starvation. Almost three-quarters of pregnant women suffer from anemia. Over half of the children suffer from malnutrition - 200 in every 1,000 die before the age of five, almost all from illnesses that would either never arise, or that could easily be cured if they simply had enough food and better treatment. Yet the land could support seven times the present population - a fact that even the 'agricultural experts' agree with.

'AID' EQUALS FAMINE

We hear a lot about 'aid' programmes by Western middle class governments and agencies. 'Aid' means help, assistance. But not when they use the word. Whether the 'aid' is economic or military, it is a loan. Countries that get it have to pay for it, or at least show that they are doing everything possible to pay it back - sometimes with substantial interest.

The 'aiders' lay down certain conditions for the repayments, an important one of which is the growing of things that can be exported for cash - cash-crops. These, as we've seen, severely restrict the amount of food grown for home consumption. One of the 'aiders' conditions is often that their 'aid' must not be used for producing goods and food for the people of that country, but must be used only to produce things for export - so as to generate the funds for the repayment of the loans.

But 'aid' does even more damage as far as the ordinary working people are concerned, for it is an essential part of the means for creating markets in the 'underdeveloped' countries for the products (e.g. seeds, fertilizers, tractors, processed foods) of the Western multi-national companies. 'Aid' is used for laying the foundations for this exploitation, since it is used to provide things like roads, electric power, transport systems, irrigation systems and general methods of water supply, training, and so on - the 'infrastructure' as they like to call it.

One of the biggest U.S. firms producing chemical pesticides and

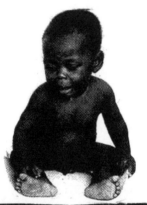

RAW MATERIAL : **HOMOCULT**

MAKES HIGH QUALITY
COMPOST
& LIQUID FERTILISER
RAPIDLY

shown here: small bottle size

other chemicals to put in the ground for growing things bigger and / or more abundant (though not nearly so good as the chemical-less things) is International Minerals and Chemicals. The Vice-president of this firm, Charles S. Denison, said at the U.S. Congressional Hearings in 1980: "I must emphasize that there would be scarcely any investment if it were not for the infrastructure, the training, and support, provided by our Aid programmes. We would certainly not be in India, and very few investors would be in any of the underdeveloped countries were it not for the Aid programmes."

PESTICIDES CREATE PESTS
Pesticides are used in such great quantities that they often actually create more pests than they destroy because they also destroy the natural predators. And the quantities have to be increased each year, over the last decade or so, yields have either remained the same or declined.

It should be pointed out here that charity 'aid' has also been used for building 'infrastructures'. For instance, Band Aid/Live Aid money has gone into it, though theirs is not much more than a drop in the ocean and really served another purpose, namely, cover-up propaganda, as has already been explained.

There are now new additional 'cash-crops'. For the big Western corporations now see Africa as an inexhaustible supply of luxury foods for their home markets - fruit, vegetables, fish, meat, even flowers, have joined the established ones of tea, coffee, cocoa, etc. All this 'development' has meant (still does!) that in many cases poor people - the great majority - have to give up more of their land and more of their labour than ever before so as to supply luxuries to the well-off people in their own countries, and to those in many other countries of the world, most of whom have far more than enough to satisfy their greed, yet at the same time the poor are becoming poorer.

So we've seen that 'cash-crops' have continued to be grown in Africa - as well as in other 'underdeveloped' countries of the world, the so-called Third World - right through the 'independence-gaining' periods up to the present day.

All the economic systems and methods of government in the 'independent' African countries are based more or less on those of the European middle class. In all countries of Africa (and in India, South America, etc.), the equivalents of the European dominant classes - equivalents created by missionaries, by colonialism, as well as by 'aid' and its consequent 'development' business - have to protect themselves against the anger and actions of their own struggling and dominated classes. So they need large police forces, and these are often just as ruthless and violent as those in Europe and America. And since none of them can trust their counterparts in neighbouring countries, they also need armies and airforces. All this costs a great deal of money. 'Cash-crops' continue to be a major means for getting it.

FAMINE IMPORTED
The buyers of the 'cash-crops' also process some of them. Processing involves the adding of lots of sugar, fat, and chemicals, all of which is put into flashy eye-catching packages designed by middle class university graduates with an Arts degree. These are then sent back

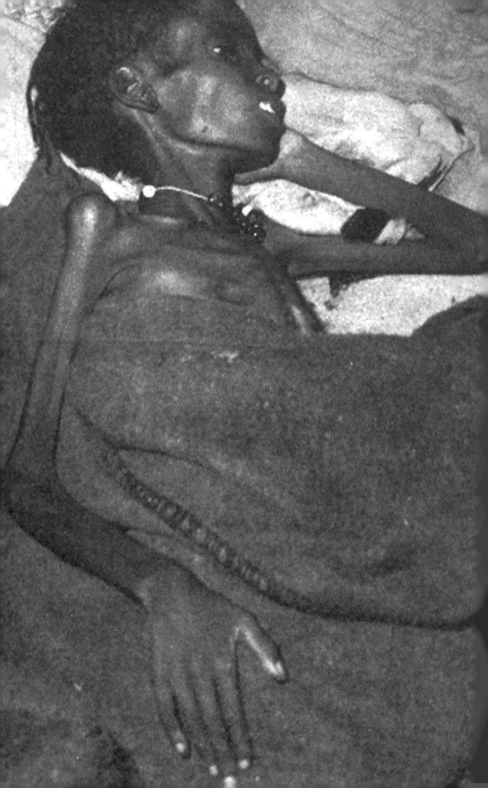

in - quite often to precisely the same country that grew the 'cash-crops' - along with other processed junk-food, e.g. soft drinks like the poisonous Coca Cola, confectionery, breakfast cereals, and so on. In 1976, 'underdeveloped' countries imported 30 million tons of such cereals. Four years later, 1980 to 1981, it had been increased by 333% - that is, to 100 million tons. Yet in that year, 1981, millions of people in the same countries were starving and dying.

To create and boost sales of this expensive rubbish, a heavy advertising campaign goes on, using mostly radio to penetrate the rural areas, and using virtually the same techniques that have proved so successful in the West. Simon Jackson, a market analyst with a university degree, wrote in an American trade journal in June 1977: "The principal African consumers are women, very unsophisticated and usually illiterate. But with the right advertising, they can be brought to an appreciation of your product as a status item, particularly with the implantation of the idea that to be modern is to be Western, and they can easily become receptive to a degree of brand loyalty greater than that in the West."

It doesn't matter to us whether this processed stuff in any way adversely affects the middle classes of these countries - let's hope it does, and the worse the better. But poor people, that vast majority, are having false needs created in their minds, and though they really can't afford it, are being manipulated into buying this junk by international criminals like the Vice President of Kelloggs International Operations who in 1981 said: "The most compelling job is to change these people's food habits."

So we find that in Kenya, to take only one example, a person can get up to 3,630 calories from a local meal made from maize and wheat flour, but only 40 to 176 calories from a meal of processed cereal - which wouldn't be so bad if people could easily afford it, but a 1 lb packet costs the equivalent of two days agricultural labour.

While in Africa millions of people go on starving, junk-food markets are expanding fast.

Coca Cola's chairman - praised by the Western middle class as a great example of their class's business wisdom - speaking about the 'underdeveloped' countries said: "The growth potential out there is unlimited, and we must get the biggest slice of it we can."

Much more can be said about 'aid', 'cash-crops', and the truly vicious exploitation of many millions of our African sisters and brothers by middle class governments and the profiteering barbarians of the multi-national companies. Here however, let's look at just one more obscene feature of 'aid' and 'cash-crops'.

'AID' AS A WEAPON

'Aid' only goes to countries whose governments are politically in line with the 'aiding' government. The 'aiders' do all they can to wreck a country whose government they consider is not in line. A case in point was Salvador Allende's Popular Unity government in Chile, South America. As is the case with the Sandinistas in Nicaragua today, Allende's government was not attempting to dispossess and neutralize the dominant middle class because as usual - like any other government which on rare occasions appears to want to help the poor, dominated majority - they were themselves mostly middle class. But they were carrying out a certain number of reforms, like that of land-ownership, which generally were improving the conditions of the great, acutely-suffering majority of people - the very poor.

Of course, this sort of activity is seen by all the middle class administrations in every country of the totally-misnamed 'Free World' as a threat to their stability. But the Chilean government's programme of reforms was seen as particularly so by that of the USA. No doubt they feared that success of such 'socialist' reformism could catch on; that it would encourage something similar in other South American countries. This, they believe, would then increase the threat to their own 'security' - by which is meant a threat, not only to the continued profiteering of their massive industrial companies such as the crap food producers, but also a threat to the 'security' of powerful sections of their own dominant middle class.

In their paranoiac fear, they have decreed that South America is their patch - the basic theory of the Monroe Doctrine lives on. So in Chile - as in several other South American countries - the United States, using the Central Intelligence Agency (CIA) and billions of dollars for things like bribes and arms, engineered and supported a military coup. Allende and hundreds of his supporters were murdered, thousands were imprisoned (1973), and a ruthless anti-working class dictatorship led by the fascist Pinochet has been in power ever since - much to the satisfaction of the bulk of the US middle class.

CASH-CROP BLACKMAIL

Not helping to eliminate hunger, but helping to eliminate the hungry

Thus, 'aid' is not only a means for creating and exploiting markets, it can also be used as a weapon to compel another country's dominant class to tow the 'aid' supplier's line. Nor can the dominant classes of these 'aided' countries rely on their 'cash-crops' allowing them more space for maneuver. The buyers (i.e. the big multi-national corporations) themselves determine the price in that they will only pay prices that ensure a high rate of profit. It's a form of blackmail; for they've already got contingency plans to deal with any increase in 'cash-crop' prices - or any other situation, such as 'political instability' caused by, say, a coup or an uprising - that would interfere with this rate of profit.

SO WHAT?

All this - all that's been said above about Africa in particular - is the situation which Geldof and all those involved with him, even those who contributed to the various 'aids', are guilty of trying to cover up. Talking of his smoke-screen 'aid campaign' in the TV programme 'Pebble Mill At One' (BBC1, 7.3.86.), Geldof said that it "puts an intolerable pressure on governments to act." An intolerable pressure? Apart from their deathly silence on all the causes of famine described above, neither Geldof nor any of his cohorts have even mentioned another middle class crime, namely, that while all the Band Aid cover-up was going on, there was a 'food mountain' stored by the countries of the so-called European Economic Community valued at £8,700 million - and still mounting; that even just the cost of storing some of the food in this country (which included 15 million tons of grain, and 35,000 tons of butter) is near £19 million per year. And the same storing of massive amounts has been going on in the USA and Japan. Some 'intolerable pressure'!

Not only was it no pressure at all, but it was a vehicle which they accepted gratefully and used with well-oiled ease to their own advantage. It was a dirty, squalid, hypocritical crime, and one made no less so by any of those who plead ignorance of what they were actually involved in by in any way supporting it - for they were in fact accomplices.

GELDOF ONLY AN 'AID'

It ought to be clear that Geldof has only been used by me as a symbol, as an example - not because he's necessarily as bad or worse than any other middle class opportunists, but because the media puppeteers tried to turn him into a puppet saviour, which not only was lapped up by the majority of his class, but also made him well known to most people, hence an 'aid' in highlighting the sordid behaviour of his class.

We saw the sickening spectacle of virtually the whole Establishment flinging its arms around him. We saw politicians, churchmen, industrialists, royalty, the show-biz mob, and of course the Press gang, all using The Great 'Aids' Cover-up to their own particular advantage - from easing their feelings of guilt to outright mercenary exploitation. It's already been mentioned how Dan Hovicky, Division Manager of the big American multi-national A.T. & T., blew the gaff (p.70) - and there were many more who kept quiet about their real reasons for involvement. There were those near-fascist newspapers the Daily Star and the Daily Express who, along with an extreme right-wing American organization called World Vision, financed Geldof's trips to Ethiopia and the Sudan - 'fact-finding' they called it. But it was nothing more than personal publicity for Geldof, and a sales-promotion gimmick for the newspapers.

No doubt the question will still be asked, 'But aren't you nevertheless going a bit over-the-top about a person who is no more than an absolute no-no, a nerd, a wally?' Well, these descriptions fit a large number of middle class people, not least many of those in their 'top ranks'. But powerful buffoons are no less our enemies. They and their class have managed to keep our class imprisoned throughout its history. And although we can break out of the prison, the problems involved are great. The vast majority of working class people have known nothing else other than being the underdogs, the losers, bossed around, told what to do, made to think themselves inferior. It's therefore going to be no simple thing to overcome and shake off such conditioning.

Being a dominated class, many among us are racist, sexist, believe that there must be 'leaders', believe in the hierarchical way of organizing things, have illusions about the need for political parties, parliament, general elections, and so on. All this is part of the prison. And I must repeat, it cannot be otherwise - for if this were not the case, we would not be a dominated class, and the middle class would not be the dominant one.

All this also contributes to a fear of freedom. Why else are some members of our class attracted - or rather, distracted - into middle-class-styled and middle-class-run organizations or parties like Militant, SWP, WRP, and the others? How else can we account for them believing that, through such organizations, they are moving in the direction of 'the emancipation of the working class'? Why else are they not able to see that to go into such organizations is not merely a way of abandoning the struggle, but is also adding weight to an illusion, thus contributing to ensuring failure? If they are unable to overcome this fear, it would be less damaging to the struggle if they went for the attraction of 'the quiet life', of doing nothing, of becoming a political cabbage. Some have done so - and, though in a negative way, have therefore contributed to the struggle.

Let's be quite clear, we must put no reliance whatever of any kind of middle class people helping us to break out of the prison. The few middle class 'liberals' who, as was said (p.67), "have nothing to look backward to with pride, and nothing to look forward to with hope," may arouse pity. OK, pity them. But a group/organization that is really, unequivocally, and determinedly concerned with 'the emancipation of the working class', if it is to have any chance of success, must only allow middle class people to do purely mechanical jobs, like 'technical adviser', 'computer programming', etc. - and even then, a very strict watch should be kept on them - in other words, use them like you would use, for example, a textbook or computer. Better still, tolerate them only to make the tea and clean the toilets.

LOOK BACK WITH PRIDE - AND ANGER!

We, however, do have something to look backward to with pride. The working classes everywhere have, throughout their existence, struggled and fought against oppression, have made some gains, and lost many battles, but have never given up, have never been totally defeated.

But we should also 'look back in anger', though only briefly - just long enough to see what has been done to our class, and what class of people did it. Look back just long enough to see that, despite decades of intensive political activity by working class people, we are no nearer 'emancipation' than ever we were; look back in anger just long enough to realize that there must be a very fundamental reason for this; look back in anger at all the political parties and groupings who have said they are concerned with 'the emancipation of the working class' - at the class of people who ran, and are still running, these kinds of parties and organizations; look back in anger and see how we have been blindfolded and duped into believing that middle class people could or would either lead us or help us to free ourselves; look back and clearly see that the reason for our failure has nothing to do with having the wrong 'leaders', but has everything to do with having 'leaders' at all; look back and see how they have concealed the truth about who our true enemies are.

Then we can look at the present, at a situation where we are still the dominated class. Then let us in anger determine that no longer shall we allow them to conceal it; no longer shall we allow them to persuade us that the State and Capitalism are our enemies, for we shall see these things for what they are - institutions created by the middle class; means through which they exercise and maintain their power and dominance over us; institutions that we shall dispense with at the same time as we dispense the class of people that created them. Let us in anger determine that from now on we shall not only actively ignore them, but we shall also actively ensure that we in no way allow them to take any but a subordinate role in at last setting out to free ourselves from the domination of their class. To do so, we must start looking for new ways - certainly not ways that have been used and have clearly failed.

FAILED THEORIES

All political 'revolutionary' theories to date which claim to be concerned with 'the emancipation of the working class' come into the 'failed' category. Throw them all out, 'consign them to the scrap-heap', together with all the middle class 'revolutionaries' who have propagated such theories, and all those who continue to do so. That the middle class are the dominant class in this society is not a theory. A theory is 'a supposition explaining something'; an exposition of the general principals of, say, a science.

'A rose is a rose is a rose is a rose.' It is not a theory of a rose. Likewise, that the middle class is the dominant class and therefore our enemy, is not a theory. It is a fact. So let's look for those new ways - ways based on the recognition of this fact and hatred of this enemy.

Hatred is good, is positive, is essential. Hatred of what is rotten is the spur to getting rid of it.

LOOK FORWARD TO SUCCESS

We working class people do also have something to look forward to with hope - provided we become dedicated to and resolute in the pursuit of 'emancipation', and confident in eventual success. We must not allow ourselves to be side-tracked by the false bourgeois notions of 'democracy', 'justice', 'fair play', 'tolerance'. Their 'democracy' and 'justice' ensure their dominance; they make the rules for their 'fair play', and they demand that we tolerate the rottenness and suffering they have created. We must act by our own rules, we must decide what is just, and we must be totally intolerant of their remaining the dominant class.

The middle class is degenerate and morally decadent - removal from their dominant position is long overdue. We must at last become unmanageable, uncontrollable, ungovernable, by them or anybody else.

EXPOSE THE TRUE ENEMY

There will doubtless be working class people - some politically active - who agree that our situation is generally how it has been described here, but who may be pessimistic due to the enormity of the problems involved in changing it. There are no rational grounds for such pessimism. The means for achieving 'the good life' do exist. But I am saying no more about what should and should not be done - the rest must be decided upon by those who are determined on positive action, who have broken out of the conditioning that created the need to be told what to do, and who are therefore able to think for themselves. For they will be able to think out new means, and find new ways of doing the first and most important task, that of exposing the situation explained here to those of our class who are not yet fully aware of it - and then propose further means and ways for changing it.

There is no blue-print for what should be done, nor should there be one. Action will take different forms in different places and in different conditions. As long as the middle class, and their attitudes and ideas, are strictly kept out, progress will be made. We know that they, through their political, economic, and social systems, have been able to recuperate - i.e. take over and use to their own advantage - anything, from political parties to punk music, that appeared to threaten their dominant position. But they cannot 'recuperate' activity by working class people who are themselves alone dedicated and committed to their own emancipation.

Earlier, it was said that the situation for the working class in Britain is worsening. The transition towards a much more authoritarian and fascist-like way of running this society has been going on since the beginning of the 70's - and it will continue to get tougher. This transition has been moving more quickly in some countries. Its more gradual slower pace in this country is due to a degree of class-consciousness - to the awareness and strength of British working class people. We must now become stronger still, and stop this drift.

WHY THE REVOLUTIONARIES HAVE FAILED

FOREWORD

Although this pamphlet is essential reading for all who are concerned and distressed about why the working class is no nearer to freedom than ever it was, it is addressed specifically to members, supporters and sympathisers of political groups such as Black Flag, Direct Action Movement, Counter Information, Class War Federation, Subversion, Anarchist Communist Federation, and the Anarchist Worker's Group. We shall refer to then collectively as the libertarian-communist-anarchist-social revolutionaries - more detailed reasons for which will become clear later.

Obviously, since there are so many separate groups, there are a number of disagreements between them, but it is not these that we are concerned with here. Nor are we concerned here with the 'political positions' on which, as far as we know, they are all agreed and with which we too agree.. For example, that 'the emancipation of the working class is the task of the working class themselves'; that they must not put any trust in leaders or political parties; that such 'emancipation' (1) requires a revolution which is more than likely to be violent; and that the rest of the so-called Left, from the Labour Party through to the Marxist-Leninist/ Trotskyist parties and groups, are obstacles to these aims.

However, there are other 'political positions' on which all the libertarian-communist-anarchist-socialist revolutionaries are also agreed, but with which we most emphatically do not agree.

While it may be said that these 'revolutionaries' are good at describing the rottenness of this society and the plight of the working class, when it comes to who is causing it - who, in other words, are the enemies of the working class - they are vague and obscure. They keep telling us that our enemies are The State, Capitalism and The Ruling Class. Smash The State!, Smash Capitalism!, Smash The Ruling Class! they scream all over the place. And they continually tell us that to do this we need Democracy, Socialism and Anarchism. (2) In fact, people have become so used to seeing these words liberally spread throughout lefty texts that they have simply become 'part of the furniture' - to the extent that whether they really mean anything is not questioned or even thought about.

We don't believe that these terms ever had a distinct meaning, and therefore never could have had a meaning clearly understood by the working class. But this is not the point. A serious examination of them will show that today they are obscure and meaningless, and their habitual use causes analyses and ideas with potential to benefit and advance the struggle, to be ignored by the very people a 'revolutionary movement' (3) needs to recruit.

This pamphlet is a more detailed critique of wrong 'political positions' resulting from a use of terminology that so far has been fairly successful in concealing crucial realities. The most crucial and important of these is the true identity of the class who keep the working class suppressed. We shall show clearly and incontrovertibly who, what class, these people are.

This pamphlet should, therefore, provoke positive and constructive debate and can be an important contribution to the discussion going on about the way forward in at last building an effective working class 'revolutionary movement'. But it can only do so provided it is given honest and careful consideration by all who genuinely want such a 'movement', a number of whom surely must be connected with the groups mentioned above.

AN EXAMPLE

Some while ago a magazine appeared which, although reasonably well written, had all the political defects we want to draw attention to. It was called 'Socialism From Below', published by the Anarchist Worker's Group. As it was also subtitled 'Discussion Forum', Andy offered to write an article criticising the magazine. Since the AWG probably didn't know him, it was pointed out that although he had written a number of political articles and pamphlets over the years, he was perhaps best known as the author of a recently republished book; HUNGARY 56. (4)

David Luton of the AWG replied by return-post saying they welcomed criticism, so please send the article.

We shall give in some detail what then ensued, not because the AWG are in any way exceptional in their actions, excuses and arguments, but because they are fairly typical of all the groups we are addressing. We therefore want it to be clearly understood that the AWG is used solely as an example.

The criticising article of about 2,700 words was sent. After a month had passed without even a word acknowledging receipt, Andy wrote to ask why. Just on three months later (i.e. four months after sending the article), a letter arrived from the AWG National Secretary - Bruno Waterfield - to say that they did not intend to publish the article because it was too long. Andy's reply pointed out, among other things, that (a) David Luton, when asking for the article to be sent, had made no conditions whatever as to the maximum number of words it should contain, and (b) it was in any case very much shorter than several of the articles in their No.1 issue, and would easily go on two pages of their 31 page magazine.

Waterfield's response to this was that the issues the article raised were of much less importance than those they were covering such as abortion rights, and what was going on in Eastern Europe. He added that the AWG was not afraid of the criticisms and would be more than happy to discuss them - but privately, through a personal reply. The fact that they had decided not to publish the article was, said Waterfield, "not negotiable, take it or leave it."

Andy answered that irrational excuse for not publishing the article raised doubts about their sincerity - for it must have been obvious from the outset that he had not proposed writing a serious political article solely for the secret consumption of AWG members; and while it was now doubtful they would be 'more than happy' even to discuss the criticism privately, one thing had become crystal clear: they were definitely afraid to do so openly in the pages of their 'Discussion Forum'. This was disturbing because in it they stated: "We intend to let no argument go unchallenged, and no question go unanswered. We intend to win the battle of ideas through our active involvement in all the vital struggles of the working class." (This, you may eventually agree, is somewhat worse than a mere overzealous boast.) Nevertheless, Andy asked for the 'private' reply to be sent.

SMOKE - SCREEN

The 'reply', which came seven weeks later, was called "Smoke Without Fire" - a title which at first seemed a strange choice. However, on reading, it became fairly appropriate even though 'Smoke - screen' would have been more apt. Paradoxically, it made the reason for the quibbling excuses also crystal clear. So what did the article say that caused these people, the AWG, to resort to such devious methods?

We shall not reproduce the article verbatim because, apart from the AWG's claim that it is available from them on request (5), some of the original has been paraphrased to accommodate the fact that much of it also applies to the other groups mentioned above.

CRUCIAL QUESTIONS

The article began by asking: Why is it that, today, despite many decades of struggle and suffering by the working class through thousands of strikes, campaigns and demonstrations, as well as their continual daily grind and conflict whether in work or out, they are still a dominated class no nearer to real emancipation, to freedom than ever they were?

Why is it that this situation prevails despite decades of political activity by those claiming to be involved in bringing about this emancipation, despite their millions of words written and distributed in thousands of lefty magazines, papers, pamphlets, leaflets?

These are questions that have never seriously bothered the 'revolutionary tourists' - particularly the university students who go on a left wing holiday for a time then, having got or failed their degrees, go back to their original bourgeois lives.

But they are questions, the article continued, which for years have been gnawing at the minds of some who called themselves libertarian socialists, anarchists and suchlike, who genuinely wanted and believed they were working for the emancipation of the working class. Eventually, those whose brains had been gnawed away either buried themselves in communes or joined the Trotskyists or the Labour Party. Others, through frustration and despair, abandoned the struggle. A substantial part of the reason for this is what we criticise in all those who are on the scene today, some of whom are in the Anarchist Workers Group.

Since the AWG publish a lengthy magazine, they almost certainly would agree that one of the main weapons in the struggle is the printed word - newspaper or magazine - because through such, ideas about things like the sort of society we live in, why the struggle is necessary and how it might be made more effective, can be put to working class people in the hope that they will find such ideas relevant and useful to the problems and struggles they continually face.

It follows that the language used is of paramount importance. Yet this, said the article, is where all such groups have failed and continue to fail, because the communication of ideas is obstructed by words which are meaningless or are given false meanings. Consequently, arguments, analyses, ideas, even advice for action, description of problems and reporting of struggles, often make little or no sense. It is a fact that many of the people they seek to help and attract are put off by the boring repetition of senseless jargon.

The AWG and all other similar groups, keep telling us that the enemies of the working class are The State, Capitalism and The Ruling Class; all of which must be smashed, and to do this we need Democracy, Socialism and Anarchism.

WHAT DEMOCRACY?

'Democracy', the article stated, is a word which, from the Ancient Greeks onwards, has only ever meant whatever it's users wanted it to mean. So what do the AWG mean when, in their policy statement, they talk of the need for 'worker's democracy', 'democratic control', and say 'we stand for the fullest democracy of all worker's organisations'?

We continually hear talk of 'Democracy' from all sorts of people all over the world - from Right to Left, Stalinists and Leninists, Tories and Labourites, Republicans and Democrats..... And the fighting and killing in parts of Eastern Europe, the USSR, and Yugoslavia, are the result of struggles for power between various sections of the dominant classes as they attempt to change to capitalist market economies while calling the process 'a reform to Democracy'.

Some of us know that the AWG and their like do not mean what any of this lot mean. But do all their working class readers know this? What do they mean anyway? What sort of workers' organisation would be 'democratic'? What sort of election would decide who does what in the councils and committees? Could all actions be decided by a 'simple majority - a majority of at least one? And so on and so forth.

These questions are put only to illustrate that it is worse than pointless for those like the AWG to keep using the word 'Democracy' - just as our enemies do - without any definition of exactly what they mean by it. How working class people could best organise themselves in whatever situation can easily be explained in a policy statement without adding to the confusion by simply talking about 'Democracy', which could mean...... well, almost anything - or nothing.

WHAT SOCIALISM?

It is no amazing revelation that there is considerable confusion among the Anarchist Workers Group about 'Socialism'. One would think, the article continued, that having a magazine that they call 'Socialism From Below' and the several references to the need for 'Socialism' in their policy statement, they regard this unexplained 'Socialism' as their main aim. Yet in the same statement they refer to themselves - as do all other such groups - as libertarian communists, anarchists, and revolutionaries. So perhaps it is also not surprising that these libertarian-communist-anarchist-socialist revolutionaries are apparently ignorant of the fact that 'Socialism' has no specific meaning.

On the contrary, there are almost as many theories about what 'Socialism' is as there are people to write and spout about it. No wonder, perhaps, that it is used as a term of abuse and derision by the more obvious enemies of the working class - such as the Tories and most of the media - to describe the politics of, say, the Labour Party. And of course, 'Socialism' has been used all over the world by a hotch-potch of anti-working class organisations to their political ideologies: Stalinist, Nazi, Labourite, Trotskyist, and so on.

The AWG gave the impression they might have been aware that 'Socialism; has no meaning when - in the Editorial of their magazine - they referred to "a tyranny calling itself Socialist, and later that "so-called socialists have made council-workers redundant, slashed essential services, and have cooperated with the Poll Tax." (6) Yet by their unqualified use of the term, they add to the confusion in an already confused working class - a confusion that expresses itself in apathy.

In any case, many working class people have got more sense than to read or to listen to a lengthy theoretical dissertation about what a particular group of people say they believe 'Socialism' to be, especially when, as in almost all cases, it is peppered with other senseless verbiage. A system of social and economic organisation in which the working class freely run their own lives can be described without simply using a meaningless label.

ANARCHIST ANARCHISM?

Another word that no longer has any specific and clearly understood meaning (if it ever had) is 'Anarchism', and much of what has been said about 'Socialism' applies here too. There is no single body of ideas and theories called 'Anarchism', hence the groups calling themselves 'anarchist' all have differing definitions of it - that is, on the rare occasions that they give any definitions at all. Yet it appears scores of times throughout the AWG's magazine 'Socialism From Below' - 29 times in the Editorial alone.

Why do they all keep using it? One is tempted to conclude that at least some of them use the word to describe themselves and their ideas out of a kind of romantic bravado - a kind of swaggering boastful defiance. Or maybe the reason is the latter combined with an emotional attachment to the word - in the sense that some people need to feel they belong to a sort of community like, say, the supporters of a particular football team may feel they have. Whatever the reason, it would perhaps not matter but for the fact that many working class people (even the more politically minded and militant among them) are deterred and turned off by words that have for them little or no meaning - or perhaps only a distorted one.

For the truth must be born in mind that, due to generations of conditioning of the working class by their enemies, most of them have come to accept 'Anarchism' as meaning 'total chaos'. The additional fact that it has no specific and agreed meaning even among those calling themselves 'anarchists', prompts an important question which the AWG and all the others should clearly answer: What does the constant use of the words 'anarchist/anarchism' throughout their writings contribute (a) to better understanding by working class people of the ideas, and (b) to getting their agreement with them followed by action based upon them? These facts and honest answers to the questions would make an indisputable case for ceasing to use these words.

ENEMIES OF THE WORKING CLASS?

The criticism of the Anarchist Workers Group's use of 'The State' and 'Capitalism', said the article, is different from the above for it is not that these words have no meaning - they do very definitely mean something. The criticism is that the AWG, together with the rest of the libertarian-communist-anarchist-socialist revolutionaries, continually portray these things as the enemies the working class must first destroy.

It's quite possible they would all agree that some of the most important sections of 'The State' are the judiciary (judges, magistrates, courts etc.), the police, the armed forces, prisons, the civil service, the church, even some social workers could be included. In the AWG's magazine we found the statement that "anarchists have no illusions ion the State". By 'illusions' they obviously mean 'a false conception', yet the AWG shows plainly that this is precisely what they do have - for they use the term throughout their magazine as if they were quite unaware that 'The State' was established, built up, and is continually being sustained and strengthened by a particular class of people so as to run society in their way, and to maintain the kind and form of order in it that ensures their continued dominant position within it. 'The State' is therefore a means, an instrument (a weapon if you like) of this dominating class. Obviously, all sections and activities of 'The State' are managed and controlled by members of this class. It follows that 'The State' can only be 'smashed' when, not before, the working class take power from this class.

HUMANISING AN ABSTRACT

Turning to 'Capitalism', the article pointed out that the AWG and the whole of the Left always refer to it as having a life, dynamic, and motivation all of it's own - indeed, as if it were some kind of human animal. In other words, they seek to humanise (anthropomorphise) an abstract.

Hence, the AWG (in SFB 1 - Editorial) talk of issues that are central to "the battle against Capitalism", and that people should be won over to "the struggle against Capitalism." That the animal needs to eat is revealed where they tell us " the southern Ireland economy was plundered by the rapacious need of British Capitalism for food." And there are more such fantasies. In fact, there are many thousands of examples in the writings of the Left where we are exhorted to see 'Capitalism' as the devil incarnate whom we should first religiously expend our energy trying to destroy. 'Capitalism' is a name given to an economic system on which all financial transactions, production, and markets are based. Over the years, numerous so-called economists (7) of various political views have written hundreds of books and theses about what kind of economic system they believe 'Capitalism' to be and how it functions. Obviously, their theories differ widely. Nevertheless, it is only an economic system. Unlike the people who use it to maintain their power, it cannot be seen. 'Capitalism', like mathematics, algebra, or calculus cannot be touched - working class people cannot get hold of it and kick the shit out of it.

When they do take action, in a strike for example, they do so because of decisions taken which attack their living standards and/or working conditions - and such decisions are taken, either in government or in the management of industries, by members of the dominant class referred to earlier. Strike action causes them problems - it interferes with their management of industries/affairs/things, it screws up their production targets, cuts into the profits they seek for themselves in the markets, and so on. Working class strikes are therefore part of the struggle against a class of people, not specifically and primarily against an economic system.

SUBSTITUTES FOR THE ENEMY

The development of the economic system called 'Capitalism' really began in the 18th century with the so-called Industrial Revolution (8) and the rise to a dominating position in society of this particular class of people. Clearly, it is a system that principally suits and benefits this class. It is an economic system that creates and ensures a divided society in which one class dominates another. It is consequently a system that is cherished and protected by this dominating class through their 'State'. But the AWG and all the groups like them, use 'The State' and 'Capitalism' as substitutes for the real enemy of the working class - indeed they use them as a means to avoid naming the true enemy.

No doubt there are some among them who do this out of pure ignorance. But most do so because they are themselves not members of the working class. Sure, we want to get rid of 'Capitalism' and 'The State'. But we can only do so when we know who the class of people are who created and control these things so as to exercise and maintain their dominance over us, and when we are conscious and confident of our power to get rid of them.

THE RULING CLASS?

So who are these people who dominate the lives of the working class? All the libertarian-communist-anarchist-socialist revolutionaries, as well as all the Marxist/ Leninist/ Trotskyist parties and groups, have the answer: 'The Ruling Class'. The term crops up repeatedly throughout their newspapers and magazines, along with the phrase 'the class struggle' - and the AWG is of course no exception. Even in their policy statement they talk of challenging the power of 'The Ruling Class'. But just who this 'Ruling Class' is - what they mean by 'ruling', and who the people are who do it - is nowhere defined or explained. Therefore, the article they refused to publish called upon them to do so, and added that if we assume the AWG and Co. know who the working class are, they will know that they are a class dominated by another class, and this gives rise to conflict between them - hence, 'the class struggle'.

Clearly, it is this dominating class of people who, for obvious reasons, use their power to prevent the emancipation of the working class - it is they who are the enemy of the working class. And if the working class are to defeat that enemy, they need to know precisely who that enemy is. To keep blankly saying 'the ruling class', 'the boss class' and 'the capitalist class' may not be an anti-working class conspiracy, but it is certainly an evasion of facing up to a crucial reality.

If the aim of the AWG (stated in their Editorial) "to be actively involved in all the vital struggles of our class" is genuine and not merely empty words, then the timer is up for terminological subtleties, for intellectual tightrope walking, for equivocation, and for the skilful (and unskillful!) avoidance of facing up to reality.

THE TRUE REALITY

The reality is that the class of people who dominate the lives of working class people is the middle class. This is a better term than 'bourgeoisie' to describe the dominant class despite the fact that it is no longer in the middle as it once was (between workers/peasants below and the nobility/aristocracy above) since at the time of the so-called Industrial Revolution and following it, this class took power from the then dominating aristocracy who have gradually ceased to exist as a class; it is a better term because 'bourgeoisie' doesn't mean much to the vast majority of working class people, whereas they are far more aware of who the middle class are.

It is quite possible to show in considerable detail that there are today only two classes in society and that it is the middle class who dominate every aspect of working class life. But here we can only briefly consider some of the ways in which members of the middle class run, manage, and control almost everything and therefore make all the decisions that matter, and how they have tried and continue to try - with some success - to condition us working class people to believe the lie that we are inferior to them.

HOW THE MIDDLE CLASS DOMINATE

When looking at the components of The State we see that all components are of course hierarchically structured (9) and that the Judiciary - from the Lord Chancellor and Lord Chief Justice, through the various ranks of judges, right the way down to the magistrates - are all middle class, as indeed are all the barristers and solicitors. We see that the Civil Service is managed and controlled by Senior Civil Servants all of whom are middle class; that the Police (uniformed, Special Branch, MI5) are run by Commissioners, Chief Constables, Inspectors of Constabulary and so on, all of whom are middle class (10); and that virtually all the commissioned officers who run the three armed forces are middle class.

All governments of the last 150 years have been composed almost entirely of middle class people. All political parties that we are exhorted to vote for are run by middle class people, so it's not surprising that almost all MP's are of the same class.

All industries - from manufacturing, through services, to arms dealing - and of course all multinational companies, are run by the middle class. The crooked parasites who are paid ludicrously high salaries for dealing on the Stock Exchange, including those involved in the multimillion pound frauds that are always going on and that most of them get away with, are all middle class.

Oil, which is of high economic importance to this country and to most others of the world, is controlled exclusively by middle class people - as are the other sources energy; electricity and gas.

All the places we work in, and all the places we live in, have been designed by middle class people who of course never asked us what sort of places we wanted. All the so-called leisure activities - from sports to holidays - are in the control and management of the middle class.

THE PRESS

The newspapers we read are all controlled, managed, and written by middle class people. 'The Freedom of the Press' we hear so much about is nothing more than the freedom of these people to run the Press in their way for their ends, which are to increase their wealth and to propagate their views, their ideas, their 'culture', so as to help reinforce and sustain their dominant position in society.

The people who run the BBC, and all those who own, manage, and run the television companies, are middle class - and they do so for the same ends as those who run the Press. The TV programmes working class people watch - whether news, documentaries, drama, comedy, soaps, sit-coms, music, quiz-games, or adverts - are chosen, written, produced, presented, and acted in by mainly middle class people.

Television is a particularly influential and effective medium in conditioning working class people to see themselves, society, and the world, in a certain way - and that way is through the eyes of the dominant class. The precise form of this conditioning is not always glaringly apparent, nor is it always consciously planned. It doesn't need to be. But a careful examination and analysis of the programmes leaves no doubt that, through their eyes, we are clearly being led to believe what they themselves believe - even if sometimes only by subtle implication - namely that they are superior to us.

EDUCATION

The education system plays a similar role to that of television, though it's probably even more pernicious. Working class children are 'educated' (as indeed their parents and grandparents have been) in school buildings designed and equipped by middle class people, where what is to be taught, how and when, is decided by middle class people - and it is they who compose the top administrators down to virtually all the teachers.

'Education' in schools where the majority of pupils are working class is a prepackaged commodity forcibly fed to these young consumers through a nationalised system of distribution, and where 'achievement' is measured by the degree to which these consumers swallow, digest, and regurgitate the package. It is a system which curbs, and in many cases, kills a child's natural ability and eagerness to learn.

It is a system which actively discourages working class children from thinking, other than very superficially, about how and why society is run the way it is - a system that in no way could lead them to conclusions about their position in society that might motivate a desire to effectively challenge the dominance of the middle class. On the contrary, it is an education system that leads them, as it is intended to, in the opposite direction - into obedience, into accepting their lot in life, into accepting that it's 'natural' for the middle class to be the dominant one, into deference and respect for their middle class 'superiors', into believing themselves inferior.

REMOVING 'CONSCIOUSNESS'

A psychological theory of the German middle class fascists (11) was that by constantly telling a class or race of people they are inferior, they will eventually accept it as a fact. But the middle class have since been more cunningly calculating than that and have gone a step further. Because the majority of them are contemptuous of the working class and believe their own propaganda about their superiority, they arrogantly think their dominant position ensures the best possible way of organising society. Therefore, through the media and the education system, they seek to remove altogether from the minds of working class people even whatever awareness they have of being a dominated class - and it is this awareness which is at the root of what we call working class consciousness. This, if substantially achieved, would obviously remove the constant threat of the working class struggling for 'emancipation'. And here too, it must be admitted, they have had some degree of success.

FIGHTING WINDMILLS

The article then asked again the questions that began it, and concluded with some more - questions which all those this pamphlet to should clearly answer.

If you really believe we working class people are involved in 'the class struggle' - a phrase which appears many times throughout your newspapers and magazines (12) - then what class are we struggling against? Who are they? Where is this 'Ruling Class' you are always on about? While the middle class are busy deciding, managing, controlling, and running everything, what's this 'Ruling Class' doing? Is it because none of you will unequivocally answer these questions that you are compelled to hide behind a smoke-screen of pseudo intellectual jargon and meaningless terminology?

It's your refusal to answer these questions that leads to the suspicion of dishonesty rather than ignorance - a dishonesty resulting in the demand that we working class people do what the Left has been asking us to do for over a century: become Don Quixotes and go out to fight windmills. This is a crucial part of the answer to the crucial question of why the working class are still a dominated class no nearer to freedom than ever they were.

The AWG make the grand claim that they "intend to win the battle of ideas" and "make anarchist ideas the leading ideas in a victorious workers' revolution". (Editorial - SFB No.1) Many of you would perhaps make a similar claim. Yet the perspective today for such a revolution is far from clear, for the evidence of working class consciousness and effective militancy is very thin, whereas the confident dominance of the middle class - as well as the thriving mediocrity and squalor of their ideas, values, and culture - appears to be as strong as ever.

So what use are ideas that claim to be concerned with enabling the working class to take power if those putting forward such ideas cannot or will not clearly define the main obstacle to power and emancipation?

THE PRIVATE REPLY

As was said earlier, the AWG 'Reply' was aptly called 'Smoke Without Fire'. True, there was no fire, but smoke there certainly was - great thick clouds of it. Yet, paradoxically, it made clear the real reasons why the AWG had refused to publish the article. It did not even attempt to deal with the criticisms one by one as set out in the article. As for answering them, anything that by some stretch of the imagination could be termed an attempt to do so, had to be searched for amongst a scattered jumble of lefty pseudo-intellectual jargon that amounts to little more than a meal of very old sawdust. It was also sprinkled with some quite ridiculous accusations.

To sort the 'Reply' into some kind of order and to translate the jargon into what these 'anarchist workers' may conceivably mean, is an almost impossible task because the very things the article criticised - use of meaningless terms - litter the whole piece, and still with no comprehensible definitions. But we'll try at first dealing with accusations, some of which do not apply or even relate to the main criticisms, and others based on statements that simply were not made in the article.

SEMANTICS - A DIRTY WORD?

They began with the stale accusation that Andy is obsessed with semantics. Over the years, lefty writers have often used 'semantics' as a dirty word to throw at some things they couldn't/ wouldn't agree with, yet to which they were unable to find a reasonable counter-argument.

'Semantics' is defined as the study of the meaning of words. Sure, we are concerned with the meaning of words, as all writers should be. It's indicative of the malaise of the libertarian-communist-anarchist-socialist revolutionaries that is necessary to point out that they too should all be particularly concerned with the meaning of words. For if you are writing and publishing material about the plight of working class people and what they can do about it, you should be passionately concerned that what you are saying is clearly understood, especially if it is about what the AWG 'Reply' called "difficult and controversial ideas". It is only then that the people you're talking to can form a judgement, decide whether they agree with you, whether to act upon it - indeed, whether to join you.

In a frantic search for counter-arguments, they said the article was guilty of 'easy populism' and 'demagoguery'. 'Populism' is a word that has recently become popular with middle class journalists, though exactly what it means is unclear. ' Demagoguery' means appealing to the passions and prejudices of people. Why they made these particular unjustified and irrelevant accusations we shall leave for the reader to judge.

'AUNTSALLYISM'

They then made the astonishing accusation that the article seeks to sweeten difficult and controversial ideas by giving them a label that makes them more easy to swallow. At no time has Andy said or even implied that he wants people labels of any sort - sweet or sour. On the contrary, the article stresses that the AWG (and all the 'revolutionaries') are obscuring any helpful ideas they may have precisely by their use of meaningless labels (e.g. democracy, socialism, anarchism).

The 'Reply' accuses the article of taking these 'labels' out of the context of their magazine and thereby turning them into 'meaningless ciphers'. Again, the opposite is the truth. It is specifically within the context of their magazine that they are 'meaningless ciphers'. There are many examples, but to take just three:

"We stand for the fullest democracy and independence of all workers' organisations." (Even the Tories say something like this.)

"There can be no socialism without workers' democracy." (Many in the Labour Party say that.)

"Our aim is to make anarchist ideas the leading ideas...." (All groups calling themselves anarchist say this.)

They also attribute to the article a number of statements that were not made - for example, that the word 'socialism' was lifted their magazine and compared to the Nazis' 'socialism'. This is not so, it was not compared to it. You will have noted that the article explained the various reasons why the word 'socialism' has no meaning and added the fact that this 'label' has been used by a variety of anti-working class organisations to describe their ideologies, among whom are the Stalinists, Nazis, Labourites, and Trotskyists.

So did the AWG make all these false accusations unwittingly? Was it a kind of political dyslexia? We doubt it. This form of 'auntsallyism' - imputing to somebody statements they did not make (or a belief/ opinion they don't hold) so as then to try to score points by attacking them - is the game of the professional party politicians, thus unworthy of serious political discussion. And though we shall not examine this 'tactic' further, it's worth bearing it in mind when trying to discover the AWG's reasons for using the meaningless words in question - while at the same time pondering on how the other libertarian-communist-anarchist-socialist revolutionaries would answer the criticism.

DEMOCRACY?

As was said above, the 'reply' did not deal with the criticisms one by one. The following statements - collected together from various parts of the 'Reply' and placed in sequence - are therefore what the AWG says about why they must keep using the word 'democracy'.

"Socialism is inseparable from working class power which is in turn inseparable from workers' democracy."

"When we talk about democracy we mean the real democracy of workers in their mass assemblies, committees, and councils."

"Workers' democracy is an expression of revolutionary consciousness that dictates and is dictated to by the democratic organisations of the working class."

"Socialism without workers' democracy is not socialism."

If you refer back to what was said in the article, you will see that an answer to the criticism has been entirely avoided. For apart from the statements being somewhat incomprehensible, the question they immediately evoke is glaringly obvious:
What is workers' democracy'?

SOCIALISM?

What the AWG might call statements in response to the criticism of their use of the word 'socialism' are also scattered around in the 'Reply'. But they are also virtually incomprehensible - so much so that it was almost decided to exclude them, for they only expose the fact even more, not simply that the AWG are waffling, but that they are floundering.

Nowhere in the 'Reply' do they show how using the word 'socialism' contributes to clear and better understanding by working class readers of what the AWG believes they should do to free themselves. Nevertheless, perhaps some of what they wrote should be examined.

Apart from statements tying up 'socialism' with 'democracy' and already dealt with above, they also say: "Ideas like socialism are difficult to get across, not because people do not like the word, but because the politics are challenging." This comes under the heading of 'the game of party politicians' because the article did not even imply that people do not like the word 'socialism'. It is not a question of whether people like the word - such a question does not arise. 'Ideas like socialism' is a nonsense because, as was said in the article, there as many theories about what 'socialism' is as there are people who write about it, and the theories range widely from right to left. One only needs to add the question: What are the politics of 'ideas like socialism' that are challenging? and the total futility of the whole statement becomes even more obvious.

'SOCIALISM' UNKNOWN

When the AWG make clear in the title of their magazine 'Socialism From Below' and in their policy statement that their main aim is 'socialism', repeatedly refer to 'socialism' in their other writings, and always with no definitions as to what it means, then they are attempting to use a form of political shorthand or labeling. This would not be unreasonable if all readers knew what it means. The fact that probably none of their readers knows what the label means apparently does not bother any of the libertarian-communist-anarchist-socialist revolutionaries.

So why do they all keep using the word 'socialism'? Is the reason esoteric? Is it a word the meaning of which is clearly understood by at least the members of each group? Highly unlikely. In fact, it's almost certain that each member would separately not be able to say what they all jointly meant by it.

Despite the AWG's statement that "there can be no question of equating our view of socialism with that of the Kinnockites," we still don't know what their 'view of socialism' is. But even if sometime they were to tell us it would still not justify using a label to describe it that has been made meaningless by a Noah's Ark of political animals.

Not surprising then that nothing in the 'Reply' attempts to answer the basic criticism, or justifies in the remotest way continued use of the term. However, in the third issue of their magazine, though still titled 'Socialism From Below', they did not use the word at all! Had they responded to our criticism? No, it must have been a fluke - 'socialism' appeared numerous times in Issue No. 4, still with no definition about it's meaning.

ANARCHISM?

Haphazard references to 'anarchism' in the 'Reply' began by claiming the article stated that "the word anarchism should not be used because it has been employed by a variety of anti-working class ideologies from Stalinism to right-wing social democracy." Here again they're up to party-politician tricks. As you will have seen, the article said nothing remotely like this about 'Anarchism'.

In other parts of the 'Reply' they prefaced things they believe with phrases like "As anarchist workers we argue that...." and "As anarchists we see that..." You will of course be fully aware that the criticism is not about what they believe (that would be a separate debate), but why they obscure and/or distort what they believe by giving it a senseless and pointless label.

Surely we are not the only ones who are sick of people calling themselves anarchists - from middle class 60's dropouts to the young punks who are dragged around by their black dogs on bits of string. We can sympathise with those of them who need some such 'ism' to belong to, or even those who just want to shock people, but they certainly don't contribute anything to the class struggle.

However, we are concerned with those who do appear to have a potential for useful contribution to the struggle - but why do they blunt it by their obsession with Anarchist/Anarchism? Nobody knows precisely what it means and therefore, like 'socialism', it hampers working class readers in understanding ideas about how to achieve freedom.

ESPERANTO?

Apart from an assertion that 'anarchism' is a working class tradition (which would be questionable whatever meaning is put on the word) , the 'Reply' does not in any way attempt to justify why they consider it imperative to call themselves 'anarchists' and their theories and ideas 'anarchism'.

What appeared to be an attempt at justification was where they said labels "like democracy, socialism, and anarchism cannot be meaningfully removed from the context of our propaganda and intervention with a content derived from our political materialist understanding of how society works and how it is to be changed."

Unfortunately, this statement makes no sense to us. But they also said that they can replace these 'labels' with others of their own invention - by using a kind of "libertarian communist Esperanto."

Perhaps a "libertarian communist Esperanto" might (and it's a big 'might') lead to a general understanding among those calling themselves 'libertarian communists'. But surely all would agree that such esotericism - use of language only intelligible to the initiated - must be strictly avoided. We repeat, it's not a question of inventing codes and labels, for the AWG and all the other 'revolutionaries' are obscuring any helpful ideas they may have solely by their employment of meaningless labels.

If for some as yet unknown reason these so-called 'revolutionaries' feel they still must use the words 'Democracy, Socialism and Anarchism' throughout their newspapers and magazines, then the words can only have a meaning less likely to confuse working class readers if every issue has, say, a preface clearly explaining what they believe each word means. Such a preface would have to be very long because, with 'socialism' alone, a few sentences would not suffice to differentiate a particular definition from the 57 other varieties. (12a)

This is doubtless not practicable. But even if it were, it would still not remove confusion - and surely all would also agree that it's essential to avoid confusion about the meaning and understanding of ideas.

A justification the AWG and Co. may have for continuing with this form of labeling is that by leaving the meanings vague they can employ an interpretation that suits them at any particular time. Be that as it may, the point is that ideas and analyses can easily be put forward without discussion being impeded by always having to guess what is meant by this or that 'label'.

THE STATE?

Although the same old cover-up slogan 'Smash The State' appeared several times in the 'Reply' from the Anarchist Workers Group, we're not surprised that there was nevertheless no response to our criticism. We understand their silence. It follows from their refusal to clearly define the class who created 'The State' and continually sustain and strengthen it to maintain their power and dominance over us. It is this refusal that is also responsible for their other wrong political positions.

CAPITALISM?

They say almost nothing in the 'Reply' that answers the criticism about their irrational use of the word 'Capitalism'. But what they do say is a revelation. They insist that 'Capitalism' is like a human animal for it does have a life, dynamic, and motivation all of its own. They maintain this is so because it has two motors.

By 'motor' they presumably mean a thing that gives movement. The first 'motor' is , they say, "the competition between different firms to maximise profit which compels them to extract the maximum surplus value from their workforces."

'Surplus value' eh? Now here's a Marxist term if ever there was one. In Karl Marx's famous book 'Capital' (13) - though only a tiny fraction of 1% of the 'workers of the world' have ever read it - he certainly said a great deal about 'surplus value'. Maybe his theory of 'surplus value' is summed up where he said:

"The surplus value generated in the process of production by C, the capital advanced, or in other words, the self-expansion of the value of the capital C, presents itself for our consideration, in the first place, as a surplus, as the amount by which the value of the product exceeds the value of its constituent elements." - Capital p.194

Or perhaps the AWG 'Marxists' would favour:

"Surplus value bears the same ratio to variable capital that surplus labour does to necessary labour, or in other words, the rate of surplus value s/v = surplus labour/necessary labour. Both ratios, s/v and surplus labour/necessary labour express the same thing in different ways; in the one case by reference to materialised, incorporated labour, in the other by reference to living, fluent labour. The rate of surplus value is therefore an exact expression of the degree of exploitation of labour power by Capital, or of the labourer by the Capitalist." - Capital pp.200-201

Got it? No, nor have we - and we suspect that many of the AWG members don't get it either. So it's more likely they prefer:

"In its blind unrestrainable passion, its were-wolf hunger for surplus value, Capital oversteps not only the moral, but even the merely physical maximum bounds of the working day." - Capital p.250

MARXIST MOTORS

Whatever 'surplus value' means, one thing is certain: in Karl Marx's writings - particularly in 'Capital' - he anthropomorphizes an abstract. So this may well be the 'motor' that moves the AWG to do likewise.

The second 'motor', say the AWG, is "the struggle between workers and bosses arising from this exploitation and the socialization of labour."

Do you all honestly believe that if 'Capitalism' had these two 'motors', it would prove it's not just an economic system? Would this really prove it's not just an abstract, but that it is truly 'the devil incarnate'?

Anyway, those libertarian-communist-anarchist-socialist revolutionaries who - due to their own emotional problems - still need to refer to 'Capitalism' as the anthropoid enemy which, along with 'The State', the working class must first get rid of (or as they keep saying, 'smash'), can go right back to Marx's description of 'Capitalism', with its "blind unrestrainable were-wolf hunger", for corroboration and support.

But Marx was wrong about a number of very important things. We don't care whether he said the working class must first smash Capitalism. He most probably did, for he and his mate Engels (14) were both middle class. And if he did, he was wrong - just as the AWG are wrong. However, KM isn't around to admit or deny it, whereas the AWG are. Yet all they can do in their 'Reply' is to reiterate, without any meaningful reasoning, that the 'Ruling Class' will only be got rid of after the working class has smashed 'Capitalism' and 'The State' - the questions of how and why are avoided.

Obviously there are at least a few amongst them that know what we know, namely that any real attempt to answer these questions will reveal their indefensible position. For the 'revolutionaries' are compelled to adopt and advocate all the wrong political positions we have so far exposed because of their refusal to clearly define the class of people who are the obstacle to working class emancipation - and this brings us to the by far most important criticism of all.

THE QUESTION OF CLASS

Many libertarian-communist-anarchist-socialist revolutionaries will agree that the necessary critique of this society and most others in the world can only make sense and be comprehensible - indeed, can only begin - when what is happening in them and all that is rotten about them, is seen in terms of class. Yet, paradoxically, it is precisely on the question of class that we find, not just confusion for that can be sorted out, but that these same 'revolutionaries' have put up the barricades.

The 'class struggle' they so often refer to only exists because there is a dominant class and a dominated class. All appear to be agreed that the dominated class are the working class. But although there are those among them who want to include in the working class certain sections of people whose eligibility we would dispute (which for the moment is a separate discussion), there is certainly no agreement about who the dominating class are because there is absolutely no definition of who they are.

This apparently impregnable barrier is one the 'revolutionaries' refuse to attempt to remove by a serious and honest examination and exposure of who the class are the working class are struggling against. On the extremely rare occasions when they've felt pressed to attempt to do so, their intellectual contortions and evasions have been, to put it lightly, pathetic.

The working class is engaged in a struggle and many are aware of it. But a substantial number are not aware of exactly who it is they're struggling against. Some do not even see the problem in class terms. Why? An important part of the answer - and it cannot be overemphasised - is that those that ought to be painstakingly explaining the situation are continually obscuring it with meaningless labels such as 'The Ruling Class'.

RULING?

It is significant that in the 'Reply' the AWG do not mention 'The Ruling Class' at all - and this despite the term appearing ten times in the magazine our critique was based on. They in fact only use their cover-up synonyms 'capitalist class' and 'boss class'. The reason for this may well be that the term 'Ruling Class' clearly implies a class that is doing something, i.e., ruling, whereas 'Capitalist Class' does not and is therefore even more vague. Had they continued to use the term 'Ruling Class' in the 'Reply' (as they still do in subsequent issues of their magazine) they might just have felt compelled to be honest enough to explain what 'ruling' means.

PREJUDICED TRANSLATIONS

It could be said that the term 'Ruling class' originates with Marx and Engels, one example of which is in the Communist Manifesto (1848) where they wrote the since much-quoted statement: "The ruling ideas of each age have ever been the ideas of its ruling class."

The manifesto was written in German and the word translated into 'ruling' is the German word 'herrschend' (i.e. 'die herrschenden Ideen' and 'die herrschende Klasse'), whereas the more accurate translation of 'herrschend' is 'dominant'. Thus, the corrected translation reads: 'The dominant ideas of each age have ever been the ideas of its dominant class."

But in translating (particularly subjects where politics are involved) bias invariably creeps in and, where possible, meanings are chosen and sometimes even changed to correspond better with the translator's opinions and prejudices (15). The people who do the translations (e.g. see Note 13) - and almost all who quote this particular statement - are middle class, which is of course the dominant class.

GREATER REVELATION

However, what the AWG's 'Reply' said concerning class was an even greater revelation than their earlier nonsense about 'Capitalism'. They said the article was wrong about there now being only two classes in this society because there are actually three, and the middle class is still in the middle with the working class below and the 'capitalist class' above. To use their exact words: "The middle class occupies an intermediate position between the capitalist class and the working class."

As you will have read above, the article outlined some of the ways in which the middle class dominates the lives of us working class people, and how they have tried and continue to try (with some success) to condition us to see ourselves as inferior to them. There are of course many more ways. But the point is the AWG evaded this, just as they evaded any kind of definition of who the 'Capitalist Class' are.

Such evasions lead them into various forms of hypocritical dishonesty, one of the most significant of which is where they say: "The development of human society is the product of conflict between opposing classes, therefore we must correctly identify classes." Surely you will agree that our critique is aimed at prodding all 'revolutionaries' into doing precisely this. Accordingly, we must continue to ask for clear answers to our criticisms.

So what is a 'capitalist'? It is a person who possesses capital? If so, what minimum amount of capital does s/he have to have? Where does it have to reside - invested, banked, or.....? If the 'revolutionaries' are ever able to answer these questions, we must further ask who these people are and how they constitute a class separate from the middle class? The more one goes on with this 'examination' the more obvious it becomes that 'Capitalist Class' is a nonsense.

CLASS DIVISIONS?

The Anarchist Workers showed their petulant frustration at being unable themselves to give any definition of who the 'ruling/capitalist/boss class' are by accusing Andy of wrongly defining class "on the basis of a division between order-givers and order-takers." This an outright lie. Nothing remotely like this appears in the article.

It would seem that the authors of the AWG 'Reply', being aware that Andy was a founder-member of the 60's Solidarity (North London) group, have been delving into some of that group's earlier publications. That 'The class divisions in modern society are more and more divisions between order-givers and order-takers' was a theory put forward by a French group 'Socialisme ou Barbarie' - Cornelius Castoriadis, alias Paul Cardan - and adopted by the Solidarity group. Andy never agreed with this 'theory' and has since criticised it in other publications, e.g. "This, if nothing worse, is a pretty desperate attempt to mislocate the class division." (16)

However, the AWG went on to say that the real class division is not between order-givers and order-takers, but "between exploiters and exploited." This reveals their irrationality for it suggests they have conceded our argument, because by 'exploited' they obviously mean the working class - and the 'exploiters' of the working class are the middle class!

They late expose their confusion even more by saying the article mistakenly defines class on a sociological basis rather than a materialist one, yet fail to give an explanation of what they mean by either. Now we're not going to get bogged down in such a sterile discussion that would only serve to divert attention from the real issue.

Nevertheless, since they refer (correctly!) to "bourgeois political scientists" who at the beginning of this century "dressed sociology up as a neutral political science" and concocted analyses about class "specifically to combat materialist ideas formulated by people like Karl Marx," we think a further comment may be of some use here.

AN INSIDIOUS ROLE OF SOCIOLOGY TODAY

There are today still some middle class sociologists engaged in concocting analyses, pretentiously claiming it's 'social science research', and producing 'academic' books which seek to fog over the incontrovertible fact of a society divided by class. But they also play another more insidious role today as far as working class people are concerned.

Sociology is today a practical tool used in social and economic/industrial control by governments through to multinational companies. It is a tool used in a variety of fields, e.g. military training and strategy, policing, education, industrial relations, advertising, marketing, and housing.

The middle class sociologists are councillors and informers for their class. They inform about what they reckon the working class is thinking and doing; they seek to discover the danger points - the signs when working class people's actions and attitudes are showing signs of becoming a threat to the stability of their class's dominant position. Sure, they get it wrong sometimes as the 1981 and 1991 uprisings throughout the country showed. But they also get it right. These university-trained sociologists therefore play an important part in helping the class remain the dominant one.

A SIGNIFICANT PART OF THE ANSWER

The AWG 'Reply' suggests that the working class don't need to know who the people are stopping them from gaining emancipation because "an independent working class fighting by and for itself will clearly draw the class lines in this society." But they completely omit to explain how the point is reached where the working class is "independent and fighting by and for itself" without knowing long beforehand precisely <u>who</u> it is they should be fighting - precisely what class of people they are.

Left to the likes of the Anarchists Workers Group the working class will never know who the enemy truly is - never mind about how to make the struggle more effective and the eventual defeat of this enemy. And this is a significant part of the answer to the questions which began the article.

FAILURES!

The Anarchist Workers Group and all the groups to whom this pamphlet is mainly addressed continually waffle about the 'Ruling Capitalist/Boss Class', but none ever describes who they are. The AWG had the opportunity to do so, at least privately in their so-called 'Reply', but did not even attempt it. They have therefore totally failed to comply with their own commandment "We must correctly identify classes." They have not even complied with what has been called The Eleventh Commandment 'Thou shalt not get found out.' For they have been found out. They have totally failed to show that society is divided in a way other than into <u>two</u> classes: the dominant middle class, and the class they dominate - the working class.

There is of course a hierarchy among the middle class. Indeed, every society in history that had a dominant minority had a hierarchical structure throughout - a graded, ranked, pyramid-like structure as in a suit of playing cards where every card between top and bottom is superior to those below it, and an inferior of those above it. (9)

But the AWG did not choose sections at the top of this middle class pyramid, describe them, then appoint <u>them</u> as the 'Ruling/Capitalist/Boss Class'. The reason why they avoided doing this is not simply the possibility of thereby opening themselves up more widely to the charge of being engaged in 'bourgeois sociology'. We must give them credit for seeing that it would be absolutely impossible to explain how these sections of the middle class in any way constitute a separate class - and most certainly not in the way that the working class and the middle class are clearly separate classes. (Incidentally, it is worth noting that all the 'revolutionaries' never clearly describe who the working class are. If they ever do, we're sure they will present us with more surprises.)

In the AWG's magazine Socialism From Below, a long article criticised the failure of the 'anarchists' over the last ten years and puts a great deal of emphasis on the reason for the failure being "no will to understand the class nature of society." This is an obvious case of the pot calling the kettle black, for a "will to understand the class nature of society" requires as an absolute necessity the clear identification and description of each of the classes involved. This, as we keep stressing, is just what the AWG and the others never do. It does not say much for their honesty and rationality to criticise others for not doing what they themselves don't do. Nevertheless, a number of AWG criticisms of the 'revolutionaries' are valid, particularly their castigation of the Class War group - no doubt partly because to be lumped together with CW can be, politically, worse than just embarrassing.

But as was said at the beginning, there are 'political positions' about which they are <u>all</u> united (even with the various Trotskyist parties and groups!) and consequently <u>never</u> criticise one another for: that the enemies the working class must 'smash' are first 'Capitalism' and 'The State', and then that spectral substitute 'The Ruling Class'.

Anyone who criticises the groups for this will not get a clear, understandable, reasoned argument in reply. Most will not answer at all. So it must be said that the AWG at least gave what they called 'A Reply' - even though it was 'secret' and devoid of any clear, understandable, reasoned argument.

Why this refusal to face up to reality? Could it be that the people who run these groups -

or a substantial number of them - are not themselves working class? Could it be that these groups are dominated by middle class people? Could it be that these people therefore somehow manage to blindfold themselves to the fact that their own class is the main enemy of the working class? If so, it would go some way in explaining why they are glued to this fiction 'The Ruling/Capitalist/Boss Class' whom they simply will not clearly identify and describe.

FEELINGS OF GUILT

In the past, some groups have said the working class cannot free themselves without the help of middle class political activists. For example, the 60-70's Solidarity group said: 'There can be no victorious revolution without a union between working class and middle class activists.' (16) Although none of the groups ever openly said why they held this view, it was clearly implied that the working class are not capable on their own of freeing themselves.

Of course, such a view was expressed because the groups were dominated by their middle class members; and it was this view that compelled them (doubtless out of feelings of guilt) to invent an enemy that was not their own class - hence the phantom, the never-defined 'Ruling/Capitalist/Boss Class'.

If any of the libertarian-communist-anarchist-socialist revolutionaries of today were to publicly say the working class must have the help of middle class political activists, we could discuss it. And though they never do, the feelings of guilt are nevertheless still there - otherwise, why still keep using the cover-up term 'Ruling/Capitalist/Boss Class'?

PREDICAMENT OF MIDDLE CLASS 'REVOLUTIONARIES'

We do understand their predicament. There are some among them who genuinely do want to change the power relationships between the classes, as opposed to those of them who want to retain some sort of power - through political party or whatever - for themselves. So obviously we are not saying that all middle class people who call themselves some kind of libertarian-communist-anarchist-socialist revolutionaries have nothing to contribute to the struggle. For there clearly are middle class individuals who are not enemies of the working class, and who do not support people who are. But we are not talking here about this tiny minority of individuals. We are talking about a whole class.

We must stress, however, that the predicament of middle class 'revolutionaries' arises from their inability to overcome their feelings of guilt that they belong to the dominant class - the class whose well-being depends on the suppression and exploitation of the working class. They can have no more experience of being working class than males can have of being a female in a male-dominated society.

We have seen many times the pathetic and ridiculous antics some of them will get up to (in dress, speech, behaviour) so as to try to feel like and/or be taken for 'working class'. Some, for example, will move into run-down working-class areas and live on a low income. Yet this cannot provide any real experience since, in almost all cases, they can escape whenever they want to because there's well-off daddy and/or mummy to help - or there are other middle class relatives, friends from home, school and university, who will bail them out with a loan, finding a job, or even just a 'good reference'. So they've always got a nice soft pillow to fall back on, whereas the working class as a whole have no such 'pillow', they just can't escape.

This predicament of middle class 'revolutionaries' is part of the reason why they want us to believe there are three classes, and that the 'class struggle' they so glibly keep referring to is between the working class and the illusory 'Ruling/Capitalist/Boss Class' with (as many of them imply) a virtually passive and neutral middle class between the two.

The AWG and Class War offer a view only slightly different. The former says "The middle class simply play a disciplinary role for the capitalist class." Class War's policy statement 'What We Believe' used to say the class division is between the ruling class and the working class. In the amended version they now say the division is between "the ruling class who are supported by the middle class, and the working class." The statement makes no further reference to the middle class since, says CW, it's only the ruling class who "cause all the problems of the working class the world over" which "can be sorted out only by the destruction of the ruling class."

Therefore both groups clearly imply that the middle class should be left alone because they're not the enemy of the working class.

HINDRANCES AND POTENTIALS

The questions the article began with are never asked by the so-called Left, so obviously no meaningful answers are ever given. The various Trotskyists just go on sheepishly bleating: 'The working class must be organised around a socialist newspaper that will be the basis for building the revolutionary vanguard party to lead the working class to victory....' - or words to that effect. They of course omit to say that it is a party managed and controlled mainly by their middle class members.

We know, not only what perilous nonsense this is, but also what crippling damage they have done over the decades to genuine working class militants, and how the have disrupted and hindered any real progress towards working class freedom.

But what are we to make of the libertarian-communist-anarchist-socialist revolutionaries who have so far failed/refused to face up to the realities we have been describing? When this refusal causes the Anarchist Workers Group to reply to our criticisms with such muddle and mendacity, what distortion must it also cause to the ideas, analyses, and strategies they put forward for consideration by their other working class readers?

We must, however, again point out that the AWG is only used as an example of what we criticise and condemn in all libertarian-communist-anarchist-socialist revolutionaries. Yet although they have all so far failed in their stated aim of 'the emancipation of the working class' - some important reasons for which we have given - it has to be acknowledged that they appear to be the only ones who have the potential to meaningfully discuss and propose action that could positively contribute to the achievement of this aim.

FACING THE TRUTH

In the lengthy critique of what they called 'the anarchist movement', it could be said that the AWG made some attempt at a positive proposal for action where they pointed to a number of things they believe are wrong. For example, they deplored the fact that "local groups could not break free from their fragmented and apolitical response to struggle because there was no organisational framework around which to operate...." which "means that, even if it wanted to, the anarchist movement is incapable of responding to struggle on a national level...." and is therefore "incapable of acting as the movement it claims to be. It lacks aims and principles, democratic decision-making structures, and any basis of accountability. This means the movement is unable to come to the attention of militant workers, and even if it were, has nothing to offer them."

Sounds a pretty devastating indictment. Certainly the groups must 'break free from their fragmented and apolitical response to struggle....' But no kind of 'organisational framework' or 'democratic decision-making structures' or 'accountability' will enable them to do this until they face up to the realities we expose and act accordingly.

It is absolutely no use them continuing to try to kid themselves and us. To break out of this self-deception, they first need an attribute that so far has been regrettably absent: honesty. When they are honest with themselves they will be able to see the truth of what we are saying, and will then be able to be honest with others. Then, and only then, do they stand a chance of being able 'to come to the attention of militant workers' with something worthwhile to offer them.

This AWG critique then added a statement which is obvious and totally indisputable: "If the anarchist movement is to have any real impact and lasting influence on the class struggle, it will have to undergo a radical transformation."

PREREQUISITE FOR 'RADICAL TRANSFORMATION'

A class maintains and strengthens its power, its domination over another class, through its control of a number of things - e.g. the media - but basically and ultimately through its control of the state machine. Bearing in mind what 'The State' is - what it comprises - how do militant workers 'smash' it without knowing who the people are who control it?

All the 'revolutionaries' still keep producing papers, magazines, pamphlets, meetings and conferences on a variety of subjects, but never anything explaining who these people are - who this 'Ruling/Capitalist/Boss Class' really are. Use of these terms have too long served as a means to cover up the true reality. They must at last be abandoned. To know who the people are - what class they are - who through their control of 'The State' and everything else, dominate the lives of the working class, is an absolute prerequisite to beginning the 'radical transformation' the AWG calls for. It is, moreover, an absolute prerequisite in building a well-organised movement of working class people who are resolved upon their class's emancipation.

A society in which one class dominates another can only continue thus so long as the dominated class more or less accepts its position - even if only because it sees no way out. And as the AWG itself admits, the so-called anarchist movement "has nothing to offer them" - offers no way out!

In fact, many working class people reject as 'wishful thinking' the very idea of emancipation. Accepting that the middle class knows best how to run things, is one way in which some working class people try to rationalise, try to defend, their subordinate position. This sort of apathy, and the indifference of young working class people to 'revolutionary politics' today, is due to the success of the dominant class in the face of the failure of the 'revolutionary movement' - and the failure persists because the 'revolutionaries' will not look honestly at what they are saying and how they are saying it. For no matter how correct their analysis of any working class struggle or problem, their suggestions as to what militants can do about it are often made absurd and incomprehensible by blanketing crucial realities and truths.

THE PRIORITIES

So it is clear that the aim of working class emancipation involves a struggle more laborious and difficult today than ever it was. The middle class have a tighter than ever grip on the working class who are today less class conscious than ever - that is, they are less aware than ever of their position as a dominated class.

True, their illusions in the middle-class-managed and controlled Labour Party are, despite the illusion-mongering of the Trotskyists, not as great as they once were. But they still have numerous other politically-disabling illusions - for example, in consumerism, in parliament, in the need for leaders and parties, that the hierarchical way of organising everything is the only way.... Such illusions are the result of over a century's conditioning by the dominant class.

The priority for genuine 'revolutionaries' today is not only to effectively expose these illusions, but at the same time to energetically assist working class militants in clearing away the blinding debris of decades of 'left-wing' conditioning.

Most of the older politically active working class people, however good their intentions, cannot make the essential 'transformation'. They go on mechanically repeating phrases learnt a decade ago - phrases devoid of content and meaning. All positive and effective revolutionary activity must have at its core the radical development of the conscious and autonomous action mainly of young working class people.

To carry on as hitherto, to go on describing the way forward using meaningless labels and antiquated jargon that obscure the realities, is to cripple the struggle from the start and a certain way of ensuring that the working class's position in society remains that of the dominated class.

'RADICAL TRANSFORMATION' ESSENTIAL

The failure of the 'revolutionary movement' has left a vacuum, but it is a vacuum that the new approach of an honest 'radical transformation' could start to fill. There can be no doubt that such a transformation is essential and urgent so that a real and effective 'revolutionary movement' can at last be built.

Such a movement is of course nothing if its concerns are not also international. It could be argued that 'the emancipation of the working class' in many other countries of the world is more urgent. The many millions of totally impoverished people in Africa, Asia, the Middle East, and South America, are today still enduring and facing catastrophic suffering as they have done for generations.

So-called 'Charity' and 'Aid' are not solutions. While these 'good works' enable some middle class people to ease their conscience, cushion their feelings of guilt, and at the same time enable many other members of their class to make a lot of money, 'Charity' and 'Aid' nevertheless act as a cover-up for the true causes of this massive human suffering.

It can be shown how 'Charity' and 'Aid' are a swindle which ranks high on the list of middle class corruption when examining why countless millions of women, men, and children are today still dying of starvation (particularly in Africa) in some of the worst conditions that human beings have ever endured; cold, diseased, clothed in rags, and often without the most primitive form of shelter. We can expose the lies propagated by the middle class through their news media such as the causes being 'famine brought about by drought'.

But that is not the purpose of this pamphlet.

'RADICAL TRANSFORMATION' URGENT!

The countless millions of totally impoverished people in the world are hardly a revolutionary class - their thoughts and actions are concentrated on the struggle merely to survive. They may even welcome another form of slavery that at least enables them to do this. Thus - as far as can be seen - their hopes of a solution may well have to reside in the working class of the so-called developed countries.

If this is the case, then their hopes can hardly be very optimistic - at least as far as revolutionary action by our class in this country is concerned. And though it is only here that we can hope to mobilise our class for such action, it is to put it mildly very disconcerting that, in the 1990s, it should be so crucially necessary to expose the sick condition of the 'revolutionary movement' by first saying all that we have in this pamphlet.

In addition, even if the present day 'revolutionary' groups in this country were at last to see the errors of their ways, the task of exposing the illusion working class people have in consumerism alone would involve a concerted, persistent and dedicated uphill struggle which there is little ground for believing the 'revolutionaries' are capable of.

But there is no alternative to optimism. We must be optimistic. So, despite the gloomy perspective, we want to be involved in the discussions and actions concerning the many important and difficult problems confronting us in building an effective working class revolutionary movement here. We believe we have something useful and positive to contribute - and there must be a number of other working class people, as yet unknown to the politicos, who want to do the same.

We therefore fully agree that a 'radical transformation' is essential and urgent. But it must be begun at the beginning! The main purpose of this pamphlet has been to show where and what the beginning is.

NOTES

(1) 'Emancipation' is a word that some may feel to be a bit dated. In the past it was mostly used in reference to slavery - to describe the act of setting people free from the conditions of slavery and oppression. It is used here because analogous conditions have been those of working class people from their beginning - a dominated, oppressed, and exploited class.

(2) These are 'political positions' which, apart from the obscurity 'Anarchism', they share with the Marxist-Leninists/Trotskyists.

(3) Those who say they are working for the takeover of power by the working class.

(4) Available from Phoenix Press, PO Box 824, London, N1 9DL - £3.95 plus p&p 50p.

(5) In 'Socialism From Below' issue 3, the AWG stated that copies of the unpublished article and their Reply could be obtained by sending an SAE to their national address. Yet of those we know who have sent SAEs, none has received anything!

(6) Even the AWG's policy statement 'Where We Stand' makes several unexplained references to 'socialism', e.g. "There is no parliamentary road to socialism." "There can be no socialism in one country." "We do not consider the Soviet Union, Eastern Europe, China, or Cuba to be socialist." Any copy of the Trotskyist newspaper 'Socialist Worker' is cluttered with references to this undefined 'socialism'.

(7) An interesting comment made by Marx in 'The Poverty of Philosophy' (chapter 2) is that economists are "the scientific representatives of the middle class."

(8) The Industrial Revolution is the name given to the profound economic and social changes that took place in Britain, Western Europe, and the USA from mid-18th century to WW1. It describes the process which economies and societies were transformed from being predominantly agricultural to predominantly industrial. The transformation brought great

wealth and power to a new class of people - the middle class - and great social upheaval. The mechanisation of agriculture and the enclosure of arable land threw many thousands of people out of work. They were forced into the expanding cities where there was work in the new mills and factories. The middle class owners and managers kept wages so low that women and children were compelled to work for a pittance merely to exist. Working conditions were atrocious and brutally dehumanising; serious physical injuries which the 'masters' called 'accidents' were an everyday occurrence.

(9) A more detailed study of the hierarchical way of organising everything will show that it is a very significant factor in ensuring the domination of a minority class over the majority class. But this must be done in another place.

(10) In a class-divided society, the police - despite the overwhelming proof of their dishonesty and falsification - claim to 'represent the interests of the community'. They in fact act in the interests of a particular class. While the police may on occasion help old ladies across the road, they have historically opposed, and do contemporarily oppose, the interests of the working class as a whole.

(11) After 1918, it was the middle classes who were responsible for the growth of fascism in Europe. It was they who were running the fascist parties and it was they who made up the membership. In Italy, for example, membership of the Fascist Party (the first in Europe) grew from a few hundred in 1919 to over 250,000 in 1921. Virtually all were middle class and included industrialists, landowners, and the vast majority of police and army officers. The reason for this was the middle class's fear of the increasing strength and militancy of the working class and the peasantry. It was due to this full backing of the middle class that Mussolini, after a threatened coup in 1922, was able to take power.

The fascists rise to power in Germany and Spain - though a bit later and in different ways - was also due primarily to the full support of large sections of these countries' middle classes who feared the increasing frustration, anger, militancy and organisation of working class people.

There is in fact incontrovertible evidence that Franco's fascists in Spain won the Civil War (1936-39) not just due to support from German and Italian middle class fascists, but mainly due to the British middle class's secret 'diplomatic' and economic assistance.

The middle class made up the extraordinary strength of the fascist parties at this period in countries as diverse as Hungary, France, Finland, Norway - and for the same reasons as those given above.

The fascist groups and parties in all countries of the world (including the UK) today are run by middle class people.

(12) For example, the term 'class struggle' appears 10 times on one page in issue 3 of the AWG magazine Socialism From Below.

(12a) Faced with the same problem, the Solidarity group of the 60-70s added to the multiplicity of definitions with a 10,000 word pamphlet (No.6 - The Meaning of Socialism - 1961) to which the reader was referred when 'socialism' cropped up in other publications.

(13) The Allen & Unwin 1957 reprint of Marx's Capital (from which we quote on page 11) is translated from the German edition by Samuel Moore and Edward Aveling, and edited by Frederick Engels: and further translated and edited by Dona Torr.

(14) Friedrich Engels - often described as 'a rich gentlemanly businessman who loved fox-hunting'.

(15) This, as many will be aware, is very much the case in media news-reporting - but then we know what sort of people run the media.... don't we?

(16) These were among several reasons why some in that group, including Andy, broke away in the late 60s and formed the South London Solidarity.

OUTRO '98

Though we are pleased that Openly Classist have republished our two booklets , it's also a bit of a piss off that, despite many years having passed, they are just as important today - perhaps more so. There importance is as vital contributions towards our class at last taking the essential first step to freedom from domination of another class.

The theme of both is similar - stressing the truth about who this other class are, a truth that all parties and groups of 'The Left' have hitherto either denied and/or concealed, thus undermining and ultimately obstructing any real movement towards our goal. The introductions to both books give more details about this.

We are also pleased because, being a small group of working class people, we could only afford to produce a small number of each, and there were the additional problems of publicity and distribution. Needless to say, there was no help whatever from the parties and groups of the 'revolutionary left', i.e. the Anarchists' and Trotskyists. In fact, First Know Your Enemy was completely ignored by all of them, even though each received a copy. Clearly, they thought that anything they might say would only make their position even more obviously flawed.

All of them also received a copy of Why The 'Revolutionaries' Have Failed when it was first published in November 1991. Yet only two - the French group Echanges et Movement, and the Anarchist Communist Federation here - published reviews (late 1992) , though neither group sent us copies of them. We only became aware of their existence when somebody not connected with these groups sent us photocopies - in early 1996.

The review by the middle class in the ACF was very short, waffled, attributed to us things we had not said, and unsurprisingly, concluded that the real enemy of the working class is, as they have always maintained, the state and the capitalist class - the later was, as usual, quite undefined.

The review by Echanges et Movement, though longer, was a bit of a disaster in that it was very obscure. And although it also attributed to us thing we had not said - lies is the right name for this sort of party-political trick - we could excuse this because it was poorly translated from the French. Though it's doubtful whether this was the reason for their quaint conclusion that "working class people don't need to know who the class enemy is because through their daily life, they know exactly who it is."

There are of course situations described in First Know Your Enemy which have changed since it was published nearly ten years ago. For example, in the section on the role of television where we refer to programmes long since deceased, we could give today's equivalents. Another is that Apartheid in South Africa has to some degree ended and Mandela is now President. But what we said about his role and that of the ANC has proved to be correct. The middle class (though some of them black) are still in control, pulling in the big money and living it up, while the majority, the millions of black working class South Africans, are still suffering greatly, with no signs of any real steps towards emancipation.

However, we believe that the reader will appreciate that the things which have changed since we wrote about them in 1986-87, have only changed superficially, and that our conclusions about them are as accurate and probably, therefore, more convincing.

ALSO BY ANDY ANDERSON
'HUNGARY 56'
AVAILABLE FROM PHOENIX PRESS

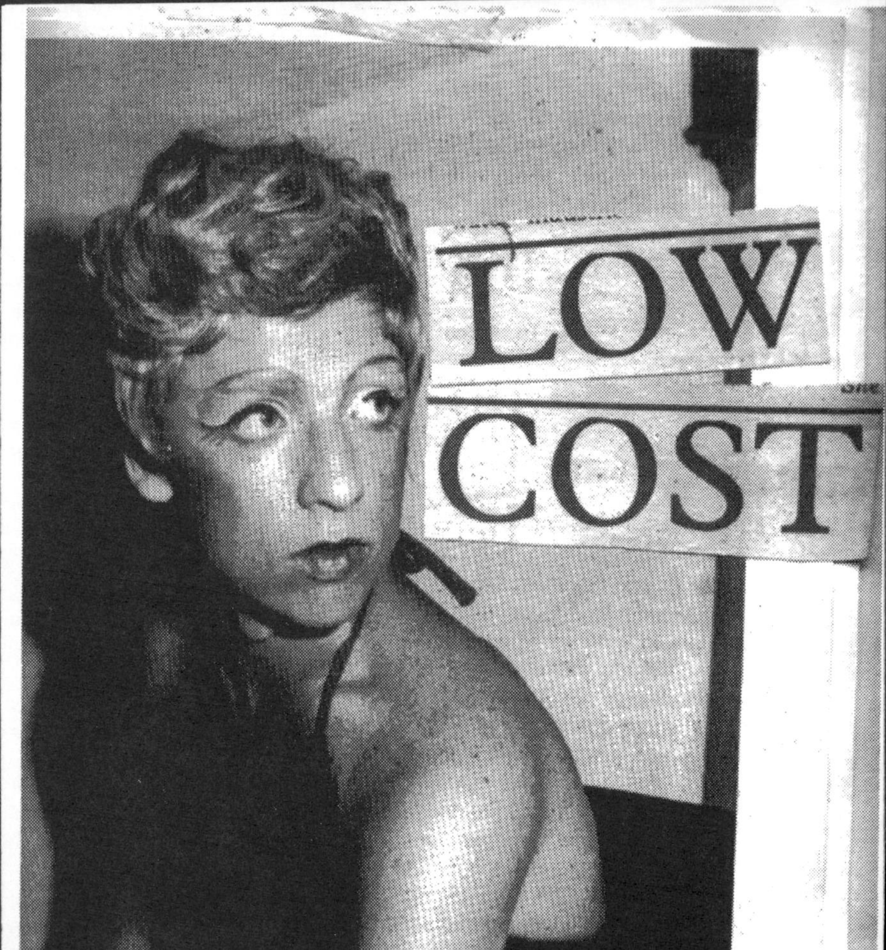
LOW
COST

HOMOCULT

No
Ability

OUR CLASS IS
MONGREL

HOMOCULT

OUR POWER IS
MULTIPLIED

FROM GANGSTER TO REVOLUTIONARY - The brutally honest story of a Black American brought up in the ghettos of L.A. to become, alongside George Jackson, one of the most intransigent prison rebels.

BAD. THE AUTOBIOGRAPHY OF JAMES CARR

First UK Publication

James Carr started fighting when he was very young and never gave up. He was a child prodigy of crime in the streets of the L.A. ghettos and scourge of half a dozen boys' homes and reform schools. In his teens he advanced to armed robbery and bookmaking, a career quickly cut short by arrest. In prison he fought harder than ever, and became one of the most notorious rebels in the seething California Penal System.

Linking up with George Jackson in Folsom, they led the Wolf Pack, which first fought its way to a position of strength in the prison race war, then worked to stop that war entirely in order to work solely against the system. With this development, the authorities were forced to increase their brutality and to separate Jimmy and George.

On his own after the 1960s in the more subdued atmosphere of the California Mens' Colony at San Luis Obispo, Jimmy transformed himself from an openly rebellious con whose actions were self defeating automatic reactions into a cunning thinker who manipulated the authorities and ultimately engineered his own release. In the process he became an accomplished mathematician, a champion weightlifter, and a wise adviser to the new generation of prison rebels.

Early one morning in 1972, James Edward Carr was riddled with buckshot and bullets in his driveway in a "gangland style" murder. While his two executioners were shown to be paid assassins and given life sentences, no motive has been uncovered.

As conditions in British cities increasingly take on an American appearance, with gangsterism seeming to be the only way out of the misery enforced by capitalism for young blacks, this timely reprint aims to bridge the gulf between the generations of rebellious youth. Because he was a fighter and not a preacher, James Carr relates the story of his life with a cold passion which allows him to illuminate the details of daily life on the streets and in prison powerfully, yet free from political polemics and moralistic complaints.

£5.95

PELAGIAN PRESS: BCM SIGNPOST, LONDON WC1N 3XX

WORKING

WRITING ON THE LINE
20TH CENTURY WORKING CLASS WOMEN WRITERS

Working class women have been published in increasing numbers in the twentieth century inspite of the many social filters which might prevent them having a voice. The particular characteristics of this voice have never been assessed inspite of the socialist movement, the women's movement and the fact that working class women are the majority of people in the world.

Writing On The Line is an annotated list of working class women writers by Sarah Richardson with related essays by Merylyn Cherry, Sammy Palfrey and Gail Chester and an introduction by author Gilda O'Neill.

As a new guide to reading this book is not only a valuable reference but also an inspiring celebration of working class women's writing.

Available from Working Press: 54 Sharsted St, London SE17 3TN
£8.95 ($20)

PRESS

THE CONSPIRACY OF GOOD TASTE

I have painful insights into the nature of working class oppression from my own history. This is a quality of knowledge which has yet to find adequate recognition in the pantheon of learned sources and yet most of us are motivated and directed, limited or inspired by just such subjective knowledge. What I learned was the central and murderous denial of our intellectual capacity which is at the heartless core of class oppression. By this means, we are, as a class, denied a community of intellectual thought through the denial of access to resources and through limiting myths of mental incompetence. The dominant culture's values and traditions are seen as embodying an excellence, rationality and taste which is beyond reproach. It is presented as intrinsically and universally superior. The dynamic of class oppression around this hub has denied working class people fulsome intellectual and cultural development. Many areas of our culture are denied altogether and what remains is devalued, proscribed and impoverished.

Available from Working Press: 54 Sharsted St, London SE17 3TN
£10 (Only available as hardback)

AK PRESS

**ULSTERS WHITE NEGROES
FROM CIVIL RIGHTS TO INSURRECTION**
Fionnbarra ODochartaigh
£5.95 ($8.95)

"We viewed ourselves as Ulster's white Negroes - a repressed and forgotten dispossessed tribe captured within a bigoted, partitionist statelet that no Irish elector had cast a vote to create..."

Ulster's White Negroes is an invaluable work for those who wish to understand how a struggle for basic civil liberties in Ireland developed into an all-out revolutionary war - a war which has claimed more than 3000 lives and has raged, with little respite for more than a quarter of a century.

The book outlines the early years of the civil rights movement, and the new wave of working class Catholics, in Derry and elsewhere, who were no longer prepared to be treated as second class citizens. It documents in detail the growing confrontation with the State, leading up to the introduction of British troops in 1969. And it records the massacre in 1972 of thirteen unarmed demonstrators on Bloody Sunday, and the subsequent collapse of Stormont.

But Ulsters White Negroes is not another academic textbook. As an activist within the Derry Unemployed Action Committee and the Derry Housing Action Committee, and as a co-founder of the Northern Ireland Civil Rights Association. Finnbarr O'Doherty was, and is, an integral part of the struggle. "From the elections to the barricades, from bulletins and communiques to maintaining communications on his bicycle rounds during the Battle of the Bogside," this is his powerful and gripping account of those historic events.

AK Press publishes and distributes a wide variety of radical literature. For our latest catalogue, featuring this and several thousand other titles, send a large SAE to AK PRESS:
PO BOX 12766, EDINBURGH, SCOTLAND, EH8 9YE

ULSTERS WHITE NEGROES

I have consistently urged all those in struggle, whether in Ireland, Britain or elsewhere, to document and record for the future the history of their own lives and experiences, for this is real history.

It is sharing the reality of our struggle and experience with those who come after us, or with those who share the same experiences in different contexts today, that we defeat the lies and distortions not only of a simplistic and sensation-seeking media, but of the revisionist, the opportunist and the egotist.

'Ulster's White Negroes' appears at a most crucial period in the development of this, the longest unbroken stage of resistance on this island. While the period covered by the author is essentially that leading up to Bloody Sunday, it is a timely reminder of how the struggle for 'one man-one vote', 'one family-one house', 'one man-one job' became again a demand for an end to British control of Ireland, and self-determination for the Irish people.

It clearly abolishes the pretence that violence in these Six Counties is the cause rather than the result of the problem, and demonstrates the consistent efforts from the community to redress non-violently the injustice of its suffering and protect itself from the violence of the State.

Having read 'Ulster's White Negroes', the reader might well conclude that asking nationalist working class people to recognise 'unionism' as a tradition having equal validity with their own is like asking the Afro-Caribbean, Asian, Indian or Chinese population of the 'United Kingdom' to accord the same dignity to racism.

Finnbarr O'Doherty has, I believe, spent some four years researching and collecting the primary source material for this book, work involving digging out dusty minutes of meetings from plastic bags in the back cupboards, hours in getting and comparing press clippings, and interviews with ordinary people who remember but whom others forgot to ask.

I hope his work inspires others to do likewise.

The events outlined herein, when the history of this whole period is written (devoid of censorship and revisionism) will provide a major part of the explanation of subsequent developments.

In understanding what life was like under the old Stormont regime, the reader will better appreciate the apprehension with which the 'natives' view any political devolution of power to the Northern State and a resurrection of Stormont in any re-vamped version.

Like many of our contemporaries, Finnbarr and I grew up with the struggle, matured with it, and still are young enough in the natural sequence of life to live to see it concluded.

I suspect both of us are born in the 'mould of dissidence' and will continue to organise and agitate in the new dawn.

May both of us, and all those we hold dear, live to see the day. If we don't, may those who come after us read, learn, know and continue to struggle for social justice, equality and human dignity.

Questioning the orthodox view that it is powerlessness that leads to serious criminal behavior, Steven Box focuses on the serious crimes committed by those in positions of power and privilege, particularly in government agencies and multinational corporations.

On the occasions when corporate negligence, indifference, or apathy does not result in employees, consumers, or the public being killed, it often leaves them seriously injured or ill. Thus in Britain from 1973 to 1979 there was an annual average of 330,000 non-fatal accidents at work. The vast bulk of these were not caused by employees' carelessness or stupidity but by the conditions under which they are obliged to work. These put pressure on employees' to take risks - even violating the corporation's own safety standards. But in this contradiction between productivity and safety, between speed and conformity to regulations, which does the corporation prioritize? A clear answer is given in Carson's (1981) analysis of the other price paid for North Sea Oil. He claims that when oil companies were faced with the contradictory demand for speedy exploration and extraction and the requirements of safety they, with successive British governments' blessing, chose speed. Consequently most accidents, and there were nearly 500 of them during the 1970s, were not the result of employee thoughtlessness but emerged directly out of the contradictory demands made upon the workforce. Also during the period 1973-79, there was an annual average of nearly 14,000 persons diagnosed as suffering from an occupationally-induced disease. The number of persons injured or made ill at work far exceeds the number against whom indictable crimes of violence, including rape and indecent assault, were committed. Thus in 1977 over 340,000 persons at work in the UK suffered through accidents and occupationally induced ill health compared with 93,500 persons victimized by indictable crimes of violence. If we multiply the former figure by a factor of two to obtain a roughly comparable population at risk size, we arrive at a ratio of seven to one in favour (*sic*) of work-induced avoidable suffering. The magnitude of this ratio, rather than the exact validity of the aggregate figure on which it is based, ought to be stressed , for it reveals just how much more objective damage is caused to persons at work than members of the public experience through 'conventional' criminal violence.

POWER, CRIME, AND MYSTIFICATIO

steven box

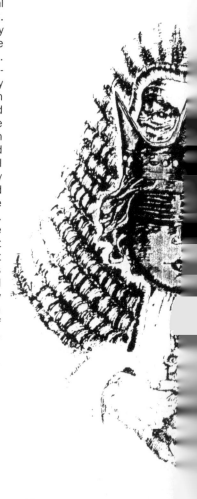

ROUTLEDGE

EDUCATING WHO ABOUT WHAT?
A CRITICISM OF THE ANARCHISTS/REVOLUTIONARIES

Working class intelligence is feared.
Middle class intelligence is a myth.
he middle class stand by the term ruling class, no doubt to avoid **their class's cosy deal** receiving any attention.
People who apologise for the middle class in politics are bad news. They try to keep the peace 'cause they want to be in both camps. This is nothing to do with whether they agree or disagree - it's just that "some individuals have **so much at stake socially, in politics,** and that is the thing they work to defend at all costs".

There's a need for hostility, and need to encourage all of us who give enough of a fuck to step away from the irrelevance that masquerades as anarchism.
ating the middle class is not about us being petty, uneducated or ignorant, it is about **understanding their role in our control** and government.
The depth of class is of no concern to those who's minimal agendas are met by their involvement in politics.

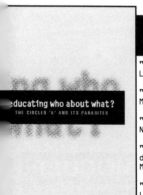

educating who about what?
THE CIRCLED 'A' AND ITS PARASITES

what they said

"Try my tasty pies"
L. McCartney aka C. Orr

"Too relevant, accessible and genuine to be of any concern to me"
Mike Balard – strange political freak – Submission . manchester

"No comment"
Norman (one of the most clueless and deluded middle class pricks in London)

"This book makes a lot of valid and relevant points; something I'm unable to do myself"
M.H. Black Flag

"Please do not read this booklet"
Leeds Class War: Brian, Netty, Keir, Dave Harvey & Alan (the scab) Huron
"Because we've been fucking sussed"

from: beb . dept 8 . 1 newton st . manchester m1 1hw

KATE SHARPLEY LIBRARY

The KSL was named in honour of Kate Sharpley, a First World War anti-war activist. Kate Sharpley spat in the face of a Royal to show her disgust at the senseless death of her brother in the First World War. She refused a medal for his supposed bravery. Kate Sharpley was one of the countless 'unknown' members of our movement so ignored by 'official' historians of anarchism.

The library comprises of several thousand pamphlets, books, newspapers, journals, posters, flyers, unpublished manuscripts, monographs, essays etc. in over 20 languages covering the history of our movement over the last century.

The Kate Sharpley Library and Documentation Centre has been in existence for the last eight years. The KSL now has a permanent base and we are in the process of creating a complete database of the entire collection. At the same time, a working group has been formed to oversee the running and organisation of the library. The catalogue of material in the library will be published by AK Press (Edinburgh).

The Kate Sharpley library is probably the largest collection of revolutionary material in England, and, in order to extend and enhance the collection, we ask all activists, groups and publications worldwide to add our name to their mailing lists. We also appeal to all comrades and friends to donate suitable material to the library. All donations are welcome and can be collected. KSL Sept '98.

KSL: BM HURICANNE, LONDON WC1N3XX, ENGLAND

ACTIVE DISTRIBUTION

Finally our third mail-order catalogue is here. For books, records, CDs, magazines, t-shirts, badges, stickers, videos, etc. send us an SAE with a 26p stamp or IRC or 1 dollar to

ACTIVE DISTRIBUTION, BM ACTIVE, LONDON WC1N 3XX, UK

HOMOCULT

THIS IS THE EVIL ART OF HOMOCULT

loud mouthed sex mad whores from the underclass sworn enemies of the state and thorn in the side of both the likes of the gay ghetto and the so called radical left. **our language is perversion**
THE GUTS OF THE GUTTER   THE SCREAM OF THE SINFUL   THE UNDERSTANDING OF THE USED

HOMOCULT: PO BOX 10, MCR M19 2XL

BLACK ECONOMY BOOKS

For a full catalogue send SAE to
BEB: DEPT 8, 1 NEWTON STREET, MCR M1 1HW

PHOENIX PRESS

Phoenix started out as a strictly anarchist publisher (the first title published was Alexander Berkmans 'The Russian Tragedy') but has moved beyond anarchist boundaries as is now more accurately described as libertarian. Over 30 titles have been published including Andy Andersons 'Hungary '56' and Joe Jacobs 'Out Of The Ghetto'. If you think libertarian publishing is worth supporting, and if you (or your mates) can afford it, then contact us about our loan / sponsorship scheme at

PHOENIX PRESS: PO BOX 824, LONDON N1 9DL

OPENLY CLASSIST

First Know Your Enemy and Why The Revolutionaries Have Failed we believe are two of the most important writings about class in this country. As Openly Classist we are very proud to be putting them out in this our first book.

We hope we are saving people time and effort by publishing this work which pulls apart the valueless political groups with their meaningless language and fairy-tale views.

From the simplest of ideas to the severest - we intend publishing works dealing with all aspects of class.

We are a working class-only project with contacts throughout Britain, and abroad. Anyone wanting to contact us then please do. Write to us at our PO box.

Class loyalty.

Openly Classist, Manchester '98.

We don't want to hear from any middle class people at all unless they're sending us money.